Breathe

A Physician's Stories and Reflections on Prayer

R. Keith McAfee, Jr, MD

WESTBOW
P R E S S®
A DIVISION OF THOMAS NELSON
& ZONDERVAN

WestBow Press books may be ordered through booksellers or by contacting:

WestBow Press
A Division of Thomas Nelson & Zondervan
1663 Liberty Drive
Bloomington, IN 47403
www.westbowpress.com
1 (866) 928-1240

ISBN: 978-1-5127-4297-8 (sc)
ISBN: 978-1-5127-4298-5 (hc)
ISBN: 978-1-5127-4296-1 (e)

Library of Congress Control Number: 2016908442

Print information available on the last page.

WestBow Press rev. date: 08/09/2016

Contents

Introduction.. ix

1. Pretense or Presence?...1
2. Unique 6
3. The Core 10
4. Indifference 14
5. No Comparison..20
6. Your Head or Your Guts...24
7. God's Clinic..28
8. Fully Aware..34
9. Mirrors...36
10. Burst Prayers..39
11. Health versus Stealth...44
12. Sorrow 47
13. Well Done...53
14. Getting in Shape 56
15. Style 59
16. Constant Prayer?..63
17. Change? 66
18. The Most Frightening Verse...68
19. Tracy 74
20. All That Trouble?..77
21. Rhinoceros...82
22. God Truly Does Answer Our Prayers............................87
23. Transition 94
24. Patients and Patience..98

25. Hunger? Thirst?.. 101
26. Steps... 106
27. Sacred.. 108
28. Tears 110
29. Complicated.. 112
30. Bone Marrow 116
31. That's Who? 120
32. Sin 125
33. Repent or Repeat.. 128
34. Incubation Period 131
35. Past and Future 134
36. Hostage?... 138
37. Ossify?..143
38. Better or Bitter? 146
39. They Can? 149
40. As We Forgive Those 153
41. No, Even So... 156
42. War... 158
43. Outside the Door 162
44. Miracles... 165
45. Miracles: Further Reflections 172
46. In the End 176

To my wife, Jeanie; my daughters, Dana, Kim, Jody, and Rachel; and my mother, Gini, all of whom were irreplaceably instrumental to my writings regarding content, editing, personal encouragement, and support. They are the loves of my life.

Unending gratitude must go to Gregory Burch of Hawthorne Inn in Concord, Massachusetts, without whom this book would not exist. Not only did he guide me unerringly in its composition, offering the sagest of advice even to the point of changing the fundamental direction of my writings, but he resurrected my enthusiasm at a time when discouragement almost made me give up the whole affair. Gregory, you are a godsend—literally and figuratively!

Among the many friends who helped along the way, special thanks go to David Morrow, Steve and Pam Souza, Suzie Laupp, Michelle Knox, Michelle Swift, David Bradley, John and Maurine Guth, Sharon Burke, RN, and Brad Bell for extensive and invaluable critique regarding crucial aspects of the stories. Thanks also to Sheryl Hesse, Gary Tindell, Diane and Allison Sawyer, Marcia and Frank Cecil, Tracy Leighton, and DoniJo Heinberger for their feedback and support along the way.

To those who do not share the Christian faith, it might seem trite to dedicate one's writings most of all to the Lord, but there is no other realistic option for an author who loves and is loved by Him. Words fail here, so I will keep it simple: Thanks and blessings to You, without whom life, joys, and purpose would not exist. May Your presence be known by all.

Introduction

This is not a book to be studied.

If there is any value in what I have written, it will be found while on your knees. The following pages contain a collection of stories I experienced during my medical career.[1] These stories—some unique and others ordinary—convey specific devotional lessons of prayer, the details of which are interwoven into the narratives. These lessons, however, are not primarily intellectual in nature, so do not approach this book chiefly to learn theological truths. The following pages are about devotion, not about theology ... although admittedly there is no clear division between the two. To put it bluntly, my intention is to affect your guts and your heart more than your head, and my greatest goal in writing this book is that your prayers—however short or long—will become deeper, richer, and more filled with God's presence.

Prayer is a mystery. It works not because we understand the process but because we know the God behind the process. Nowhere in scripture are we given a comprehensive exposition on prayer, and I believe this omission is by God's grace and wisdom. An all-inclusive treatise on the subject would be beyond our comprehension and likely would cause us to study—rather than practice—prayer.

---

[1] The two exceptions, chapters 16 and 30, are true stories that did not happen to me personally but were told to me at different times during my career.

Instead, God provides us with certain truths about prayer—enough to guide us, to deepen our love of Him, and to keep us spiritually safe, but not enough for us to think of ourselves as authorities on the subject. This, by the way, is not such a bad thing, as our need to fully comprehend the subject fades as we grow deeper in the practice and fruits of our prayer life. Prayer is not primarily theological or intellectual—it is primarily *relational*...because God is primarily relational. In the end, the mystery of prayer is solved by the intimate presence of eternal Love, not by the theological answers of eternal Mind.

Prayer to our souls is like breathing to our bodies: without breathing we die physically, and without prayer we die spiritually, however gradual that latter process might be. That being said, breathing was not created by God only to keep us alive—as if mere physical existence were the goal of our lives—but was designed to sustain us during fulfilling, enjoyable physical activities such as climbing a mountain, singing a love song, conversing with friends, defending the needy, taking a deep breath of fresh pine-scented mountain air, or helping resuscitate someone in cardiorespiratory arrest. In other words, it is the *rewards* of breathing that ultimately make it so valuable.

In like manner, prayer was never meant to be dry and dutiful, simply sustaining our faith in some rudimentary fashion. Prayer is supposed to be fulfilling, to draw us close to God's heart, and to open our lives to His very presence. It is supposed to flow from our hearts. In the same way that physical breathing typically is a natural, constant process that does not require conscious choice but occurs simply because of who we are as living beings, prayer ideally should be an unceasing, rewarding, natural outgrowth of who we have become as believers.

Alas! Prayer unfortunately is not so easy, because we are not yet as fully godly as we are fully physically alive, so breathing comes readily while prayer often is a struggle. In our fallen state, prayer frequently can seem emotionally empty, especially for converts during the years after the first glow of conversion fades or for lifelong Christians who struggle with the doldrums of overfamiliarity with their faith.

My contention—and the goal of this book—is that prayer, far more than simply sustaining our faith, can be tremendously rewarding if properly understood on a personally experiential (rather than merely on an intellectual) level and can lead us to treasures of unspeakable value. When God touches our hearts with the intensity of a lover, then the real excitement begins! But how do we allow that to happen? How do we permit Him to pass through our protective shells? If our prayers have become stale, how do we find the motivation in our hearts to pursue Him with fervor once again? Last, for those who already pray well, how to progress further to even deeper prayer?

The answer, of course, is that only God can accomplish those goals ... but such an achievement *only* happens when we taste His presence and when we get our misconceptions out of the way of His personal touch—and what better way for us to learn how to do this than through stories?

Because stories get under our skin. Through the tales of other people's lives, we vicariously experience and *feel*—we do not merely think about—the truths to be learned, which opens our hearts to His Spirit in a way that scholastic studies cannot. There is much for all of us to learn in our spiritual lives, and my hope is that the following stories and lessons from my medical career will enrich your prayers as they have mine.

Prayer—at least deep and rich prayer—is woefully underrated and, I am afraid, vastly underutilized. This is most true in wealthy countries of any nationality, where one's priority so easily can become the comfort of the body rather than the conversion of the soul. If this tendency is not true in your life, then you have my undying respect. It certainly is true in mine. Therefore—speaking selfishly for my own sake as well as generously for yours—it has become my fervent prayer that more fervent prayer may abound, and I offer this book as my own encouragement toward that end.

Each of the following stories is true.[2]

---

[2] As is customary, names have been changed, and all pertinent details (even gender) that could identify any particular person have been altered to protect privacy.

1

Pretense or Presence?

Mabel looked up at me. "No. I can't hear you," she responded. I blinked, and my head involuntarily twitched.

"Not at all?" I asked.

"Nothing," she answered, turning her head away. A further pause.

"That must be awful for you," I stammered.

Mabel shook her head and mumbled, "It's terrible."

I dumbly repeated, "Really no hearing at all?"

She gazed at me again. "No!"

Not sure what to say next, for the moment I just stared at her. Mabel was an elderly woman in a local nursing home where I volunteered most Sundays during my first two years of medical school. A wonderful woman in our church led a weekly Sunday-morning church service at this nursing home, and when my medical school commitments did not preempt my plans, I was able to help most Sundays by playing the guitar or preaching a short lesson. After the service I would visit many of the patients who lived there, spending much of the afternoon reading stories out loud or talking with them about their thoughts.

During one of those Sundays, I noted that Mabel had arrived as a new patient, so I went to talk with her after the service. In truth, Mabel did have significant hearing loss, and I had to shout to be heard, which disturbed the other residents. I therefore used a technique that physicians find helpful: borrowing a stethoscope from one of the nurses, I placed the earpieces in Mabel's ears (rather than in my own), and I talked into the end of the stethoscope that is usually placed on the patient's chest. This trick works quite well, and I thereby could lower my voice and still sound sufficiently loud in Mabel's ears. Despite her denials, she heard me just fine, a fact I tested with friendly small talk. She always answered appropriately. Perplexed but fascinated, I decided to find out why she held to her claim.

I knew enough not to confront her head on, so I approached the subject indirectly by asking about her life. Two facts soon became clear. First, she exhibited not one shred of deceitfulness. She was sincerely convinced that she was deaf, even though she was answering my questions. Second, her conviction was not due to dementia. Mentally she was fine. I will not bore you with the long conversation we had—most of which I have forgotten anyway—but suffice it to say that I eventually discovered the truth: she did not like what her family members (mostly her children) were telling her, so she decided to be deaf in order to avoid what they had to say. She started with her legitimate and profound hearing deficit, and by choice of will, she made it complete. Voilà! Can't hear a thing! She could conveniently ignore any unwelcome words.

Of course, she did not admit to this fact directly. The truth came out through long, indirect questioning, and ironically, getting to the truth of why she allegedly could not hear was accomplished through her hearing. I was conversing with someone who was telling me she could not converse! The undeniable fact that we were carrying on a back-and-forth conversation was not enough to break through her mind-set: she needed to be deaf, and that was that. Nothing as trivial as the truth was going to stop her. She could not handle what she was hearing from her family, and so, as horrible as it might be for her, she now could not hear anything at all. She was miserable about it, and she bemoaned it, but facts were facts: she would just have to live with being cut off from the world.

During the ensuing months, Mabel held to her story. It was remarkable. At some point I figured I knew her well enough that I could gently challenge her about her self-delusion. If she was deaf, I asked her, how was she able to carry on a conversation with me? In response, she launched into some convoluted justification that allowed her to maintain her claim and yet still be able to hear me. To be honest, I have forgotten the exact details of her reasoning, although I think it had something to do with my "tone of voice," but I do remember being in awe of her talent for self-deception. Having such a psychological need to avoid the pain of the truth about herself, she believed in her lie so completely that she no longer even realized she was lying to herself. It was profoundly sad.

But not as sad as later on.

Over the years, when circumstances have brought Mabel to mind, I have reflected on her self-imposed predicament. For a long time I was able to think about her from a comfortable distance, sad for her but marveling that anyone could so completely deceive herself—until one day, as my own personal devotional life was deepening, I realized that, in more ways than I cared to admit, *I am Mabel*! And I am not like her in some token, trivial way. I am deeply and utterly Mabel.

Am I ever willfully deaf when I approach God, such as when I am afraid that He might exhort me about some embarrassing character trait or some element of weakness in my life? I loathe feeling like a failure, and I never like to face my faults. Indeed, I do not like to admit that I even have faults. Or how about the ways in which I want to approach God or "follow" Him on my own terms and in my own way rather than on His terms and in His way? Or what if He needs to exhort me that I am the one who is wrong or pigheaded about some argument I have just had with my wife or children? I do not like having to eat humble pie when I am angry. Or how about when I think God might call me to do something I do not want to do? I do not appreciate having to change my well-laid plans. I also do not like to give up what I hold dear, even if it is not good for me. Am I therefore not Mabel's equal in talent for self-delusion and self-justification in my selective hearing? When on my knees, do I just prattle on and on, never stopping long enough or being vulnerable enough to be counseled or corrected by my Father? Such habits on my part are pure pretense[3]—pure "Mabel." To not face unwelcome truths about my life is the comfortable way out, but it also keeps God out. I can have the comfort of my *pretense* or the joy of God's

---

[3] Pretense: an attempt to make something that is not the case appear to be true.

presence, but I cannot have both, as they are mutually exclusive. I must choose.

During prayer I need the courage to be open and honest and to let God gently teach me, perhaps make me joyful, or tell me "well done" about something. Conversely, perhaps He needs to scold me, gently swat me on my spiritual bottom, help me face my faults so I can learn from them, or change my plans so I will become unendingly happy. In truth, I *am* frighteningly like Mabel. Perhaps we all are.

Unlike Mabel, we do not have to remain that way.

2

Unique[4]

We both marveled at the wonder of it.

Counting the disadvantaged babies and toddlers she had adopted—some with development disabilities—along with her several biological children, Carla, a full-time mother, had a total of twelve children to raise, several of whom were now grown and on their own, but many of whom were still in school and living at home. To say the least, she and her husband had their hands full! Carla was an extraordinary mom—devoted, generous, loving, and undeniably competent. As you can imagine, with so many children in the household, she was frequently in my clinic for one ill child or another, and for reasons of practicality, she often brought many of the siblings along. I enjoyed the crowd.

During one of those visits—for reasons I no longer remember but I suspect originated from some observation of her children's interactions—our discussion turned to the incredible variety of personalities that coexist in a family. This variety is as true in my home of four daughters as it is in her home of twelve

---

[4] The original idea for this section comes from C. S. Lewis in his book *The Problem of Pain* and should be credited to him.

mixed boys and girls. No two siblings are alike, a condition that brings variety and creativity to a family. Each child's special, one-of-a-kind personality cannot be replaced and is uniquely valued by the parents. There are no reprints among humans— we are all originals of a master painter. After musing about this fact and sharing a brief chuckle, Carla and I marveled at the wonder of it.

What is true of Carla's family is also true of our largest family, the one we call the human race. No two people are alike, no matter how similar they might seem on the surface. No one in all of human history will be the same as you—not just physically, mentally, or emotionally, but also in how you *experience* life: the way you see or feel events, your perception of beauty, how you interact with the world, what you value in other people, what makes you feel fulfilled, or any other of the innumerable aspects of your personality. You are and always will be, without doubt, the only one of you.

I believe God likes it that way. He is, after all, the one who created us so. And I believe He did that for a very specific reason: He wants to love each of us as one-of-a-kind individuals rather than as a collection of identical copies. Every one of us is special to Him, not simply because He considers us sons and daughters in His image, but because, in a sense, we are an *only* son or daughter—we cannot be replaced. If you reject God, He will not merely mourn the loss of a child whom He loves more than words can convey, but He will mourn the loss of a treasured relationship with a child that can never—even in the lives of a trillion other people—be replaced. To try and make up for the loss of you, He could extend the life of the universe one hundred–fold and expand the total eventual population of human beings ten thousand–fold, but it still would not work: He would pine *specifically* for you forever, because there can never be another you. In my career I have known many parents who have suffered the death of a child, and the birth of subsequent children into those families, although a blessing, never eliminates the longing for that lost child. This truth helps us understand how valued we are in God's eyes, and how none of us is even slightly less important to Him, no matter what the world tells us about our worth.

All of the above is also true regarding our prayers. Because of the unique way in which you and I perceive, value, and relate to God, each of us will have our own special, never-to-be-repeated experience of God's presence. You will appreciate different hues and shades of His infinitely rich character in ways I—and everyone else throughout history—cannot imagine, and vice versa. I believe, as C. S. Lewis says, that this uniqueness in relationship will extend for all time, even in heaven. Somehow, in the mystery of heaven, even though all of our hearts will be similarly perfected, God nevertheless will enjoy the variety of human personalities forever. It is said that we will live in heaven in perfect harmony, but the word *harmony* implies diversity, not monotony.

Fortunately we do not have to wait until heaven to enjoy this truth. When in prayer, we should feel irreplaceably valued when we contemplate that we have something special—ourselves—to share with God in a manner that no one else ever will. God loves that about each of us. It is impossible to overemphasize how remarkably and *individually treasured* each of us is to Him. Although God is infinitely sufficient and lacks nothing, He nevertheless somehow, in the mystery of His being, misses *you*—and no one else in your place—when you are away from

Him. You are uniquely delightful to Him, which is an amazing and exciting truth.

During your prayers, *that* is a wonder you and God can marvel at together.

3

The Core

Angelica was beyond cute.

She was outright gorgeous … but mainly in her eyes and her smile. A mere fourteen months old, Angelica was cuddling with her mother, who was sitting in a chair in my exam room. Her feet firmly planted on her mom's lap, partly standing with her bottom sticking out and her waist bent forward, her arms tightly wrapped around her mom's neck, Angelica had her head glued to her mother's shoulder while she looked at me sideways and smiled broadly enough to swallow her ears. She felt safe, utterly content, and unfathomably loved. The sight made my smile as broad as hers.

One of the most endearing things I witness as a primary care physician is the relationship between a young child and his or her parents. I know a thousand Angelicas—girls and boys alike—who, with none of the aloof embarrassment that often characterizes an older child's behavior, relate to their parents with unreserved love and trust. There is an intimacy in the interaction that is awe-inspiring. Not simply tolerant to be in the parent's arms, these young children are overjoyed to be there. On so many legitimate levels, the parent of such a child is thrust into the role of the child's "God": loving, providing, protecting, wise, immeasurably powerful, etc. The child basks in that relationship.

So it is, or so it should be, with prayer. In my experience, at its most fundamental level—what you might call its core—prayer boils down to two major issues: *relationship* and *trust*. Miss this point, and I believe you miss 99 percent of the meaning of prayer. However old we are and no matter how grown up we consider ourselves to be, we are all in reality, like Angelica, extraordinarily young. Our wisdom has a difficult time keeping up with our present circumstances; it cannot come close to penetrating our future. Either we love and trust our Father, or we go it alone, missing the primary relationship for which we were created in the first place.

And the contact point of that relationship is prayer.

Relationship and trust—all other aspects of prayer derive from these two. *Relationship*, in that the primary objective of prayer is to grow in love with our Father, to be in His presence. If there is no genuine relationship, then our prayers become rote obligatory duties, shopping lists of our wants, superficial pep rallies, or spiritual complaint forms. *Trust*, which arises from this relationship, in that we grow sufficiently in love that we are confident our Father always will do what is best (i.e., we have peace and can pray with confidence, even when in pain or worry). If there is no trust that our prayers are heard and that God will answer them in the best way—taking our heartfelt desires into account but also knowing what is best— then our prayers become meaningless rituals in which we do not believe, or our requests become the demands of a person who does not want to hear no for an answer. If we keep our focus on relationship and trust, I assert that all other aspects of prayer will fall into line.

Although obvious to many Christians, this perspective is remarkably hard to put into practice. Think about the time we spend in prayer: Do we *really* spend it in heartfelt relationship? Or do we just talk nonstop to fill the time? Do we ever just bask in God's presence? Do we even desire His presence? When we are quiet—if ever—do we expect to receive any input from God? Do we *want* to hear from Him, knowing that He might not agree with some of our opinions or attitudes? Is prayer just duty? Or driven by guilt? Or is our time in prayer like spending time with our parents when we were very young: fruitful, relational, full of trust, and basking in mutual adoration?

Notice that I do not describe prayer primarily as communication. I can communicate with a store clerk down the street or with an Internet salesperson halfway around the world, but that does not put us into loving relationship. In interactions like Angelica and her mother mentioned above, words are the *least* significant part of the interchange. The mutual gazes, the cuddling, the contented sighs, the head on the shoulder, and the shared smiles all communicate far more than the words. Do not limit the meaning and practice of prayer to a discussion with God, or even to praising God. It goes far deeper than that. Prayer is the contact point of a family relationship—we are, in some mysterious way, a true child of a true Father, preparing to live with Him eternally. Such a relationship begins now, not when we die. We cannot expect to put off this affair until the end of our lives, after we have had our fun, kept our independence, and "done our thing." In true prayer there is a self-giving, an openness to change, and a vulnerability that puts at risk everything we are and have. We cannot expect to be the master of the relationship with our Father.

Yet we so often try to do that very thing in our prayers, being content to keep God at a safe, comfortable distance. Indeed, one of the biggest reasons people are reluctant to engage in the kind of prayer I advocate (and I include myself in this) is that it is so flagrantly *un*safe—we risk everything. Our Lord, whom we have been treating like a pen pal, comes face-to-face ... and He is no pushover. In genuine prayer, we give up control. What if He asks us to do something we do not want to do? Or change our opinions? Or change our views regarding some moral issue? Or forgive a person we do not like? Or help that person who won't appreciate our help? We cannot truly relate to our Lord and still be in charge. *We* kneel; *He* reigns. God is not content with our warm, fuzzy comfort and nice feelings. He aims to bring joy, not sentimentality. Contact with the "hound of heaven" is no mere quaint get-together. We should pray with peace of heart but never with casual disregard—His love is compared to fire, not to a warm mug of spiced cider. *Relate* to Him. *Trust* Him. Open up to Him. Share time with Him like Angelica shared with her mother, and your heart will smile as broadly as Angelica's face did. You will never regret it.

And you will not want to turn back.

4

Indifference

Relatively speaking, he was still young. Only in his forties, Dan had severe hypertension.[5] When in my clinic, his blood pressure routinely would be higher than 200/100, and sometimes more than 240/140, a critically dangerous level that required emergent hospitalization in the intensive care unit and potent intravenous medications. A thorough evaluation confirmed that there was no curable secondary cause of Dan's hypertension, so the only way to bring his blood pressure under control was through the use of prescription medications—and it took multiple.

Dan repeatedly ran out of his medicines because he would not refill them and would not return for his scheduled periodic evaluations. Elevated blood pressure can cause headaches, and Dan would come back to my clinic only when his constant

---

[5] Blood pressure (abbreviated as BP) is written as two numbers in fraction form, such as 120/70. The upper number (*systolic* BP) is the body's peak BP when the heart gives a beat. The lower number (*diastolic* BP) is the body's resting BP between heartbeats. There is no established perfect BP level for an adult, as there is significant variability between people. Expert consensus guidelines also change (appropriately!) as newer research becomes available. General consensus at this point, however, is that "severe" high blood pressure means systolic BP readings above 180.

headaches became intolerable. I would encourage him once again to remain compliant, and for a short while he would do so, during which time his headaches would resolve—and then he would run out of medications again. I emphasized that this cycle of noncompliance could result in, among other things, a heart attack, a stroke, kidney failure, or even death. I felt like a broken record. I changed his prescriptions on several occasions just in case he was having unspoken side effects, but to no avail ... nothing changed his habits. He was never the least bit unpleasant about my treatments—he simply let things go. Not even his family's intervention helped.

One day, still in his forties, it caught up with him. Out of medications once again, a blood vessel in his brain burst due to the high pressure in his arteries, thereby causing intracranial bleeding. These hemorrhagic strokes are typically the worst kind. He was brought to the emergency room where he deteriorated quickly, so he was placed on a ventilator and moved to the intensive care unit. He never regained consciousness. After a week of intensive treatment that provided no improvement in his overall medical status, and with a thorough evaluation that indicated no meaningful brain function left, a family conference was held. Universal agreement was to remove all artificial life support and let things take their natural course. This was done. He was, of course, given appropriate supportive care, but he never improved. Two weeks later he died—peacefully and with dignity—but very young, and from a tragedy so easily preventable.

What was Dan's problem all along? As he admitted to me in the clinic room on several occasions, he simply was not motivated to treat his illness. It was not that he had a bad life. He just did not care enough about his health. Among other things, he did not like having to take medications—even if lifesaving—so he preferred to suffer his headaches. More generally, Dan did not like having to spend time and energy on his health. It was a bothersome duty that interrupted his other priorities. It was a cost he was not willing to pay. If something bad was going to happen, then so be it. I remember him shrugging his shoulders once with a resigned look on his face when we discussed that probability. He did not like having a health problem, so he lived his life as if he had none. It was not so much that he denied his hypertension—he simply ignored it.

If you are at all like me, Dan's story hits uncomfortably close to home. Health to a physical life is like holiness to a spiritual life. In today's world, holiness has become such a sterile word. In reality, it is the opposite. Holiness, when properly lived, is excitement beyond all measure. It decidedly is not the bland, boring, prude, aloof spirituality that is so often portrayed, but rather it is a dynamic, rich, vibrant, exhilarating, down-to-earth gift that brings true adventure to life—the kind of thing that, once experienced, we do not want to give up without a fight. All Christians have been assured of this truth by reliable sources. Deep down, we know it is true. What, then, is the problem? Why do we not grab for it?

Indifference!

Call it by a thousand other names, but I still believe our major hindrance to deeper devotion is indifference. In my experience as a physician, indifference is the biggest impediment to vibrant physical health. It definitely was Dan's major problem. Admittedly Dan's degree of indifference was rather extreme, but all patients—and that includes me when I am the patient— exhibit some sort of indifference toward certain aspects of their health. Lifestyle is the hardest thing for a physician to change in a patient's life, and I believe the same is true in the spiritual life of a Christian. Our fallen nature dulls our senses, blurs our vision, and leaves us with a tendency toward indifference. Left to our own devices, we naturally drift more toward spiritual sedation than toward sanctity.

Yet I think we often mistake why that tendency is true.

If you and I were put in front of a tape recorder and asked to list the character traits that most keep us from spiritual growth, I think our tendency would be to name the things that we hate most in ourselves: perhaps selfishness, pride, pettiness, our most embarrassing shortcomings, etc. Those traits are indeed impediments, but when it comes to the question of spiritual *stagnation*, my contention is that indifference overshadows them all. We simply have been lulled into complacency.

In Dan's case, it did not bother him that he was indifferent to his health. To put it another way, he was indifferent to his indifference. He shrugged it off when I brought up the subject. I am not sure why. It cost him everything. It was a perspective in him that I tried many times—without success—to change, but it was purely his choice. He did not want health badly enough.

In your and my case, we face the same question regarding holiness as Dan faced regarding his physical health: Do we want that? Really? Fully? Stop and reflect on this for a moment. The joy of holiness is surprisingly within reach ... but only *if* we are willing to reach for it. I believe that all other questions regarding holiness are secondary to these four astoundingly simple words: "*Do I want that?*" Every chapter in this book assumes from the outset that you want to be holy at least on some level to some degree. But that does take work, time, some prioritizing, and a conscious decision to want it. Holiness does not soak into our lives by mistake. We must *choose*.

But—in our defense—is that so easily done?

If someone were to ask me whether I want to be holy, my honest response would be "Well, yes! … (uncomfortable pause) … but no, often not." I would speak the first half of that answer loudly and confidently with my head held high, but the second half I would confess under my breath with slumped shoulders and my head hanging down. Whether we want to be holy is one of the most important questions of our lives. But here we have to be brutally honest with ourselves: Do we *always* want that? At every moment? If your answer to that question is yes, then your spirituality far exceeds my own, and I have little to offer you.

On the other hand if you, like I, answer with that embarrassed and mumbled version of "… no, often not," then I ask a more helpful question: Do you *want* to *want* holiness? The distinction here is crucial. It is, in my opinion, what separates the true Saints from the rest of us. It is the key to the passion of King David's repentance. And it is what helps us get up when we fall.

I think all Christians want to be holy at some point on some level. But none of us in our fallen state, Saint or not, *always* wants holiness. We can be a lazy lot. Concupiscence (our current fallen state due to original sin) is no mere annoyance. We often are content with token faith, trying to squeak by with a passing grade—making it to heaven while holding onto as many worldly pleasures as we think we can get away with; letting God be a part-time God while we maintain as much control over our lives as we can. We punch in our time card for our spiritual workday, but we like the hours to be minimal, and we do not like to work overtime. We give a tithe of our attention to God but prefer that He not interfere with the rest of our day. So the likelihood is that you and I at times find ourselves *not* wanting holiness. We want something else more. The question for us then becomes, are we content with that?

I hope not.

The fact that we do not want to be holy 100 percent of the time is not so bad. Every human being, Saint or otherwise, shares that shortcoming. But if we are content with that fact, *that* is when we are in trouble. And the spiritual costs can be dire. In my own life, it is remarkable how easily I slip into spiritual complacency. But that bothers me! I want things to be otherwise, and that is what turns me around. At those times I hate that I am complacent. I am *not* indifferent to my indifference. When I am spiritually lazy or indifferent, my soul aches inside, as I miss the Lord's intimate presence that I have grown to enjoy. Dan's headaches were a gift to him, in that they warned him of his ill health. In the same way, my aching soul warns me of my spiritual complacency. Dan ignored his warnings.

Do I do the same?

5

No Comparison

She reached upward across her chest with her right hand and scratched her left shoulder.

Such a seemingly trivial achievement. So simple.

But the feat was performed by Shari, and for her it was monumental.

Shari was in her late forties and because of neglected high blood pressure, had suffered a stroke the year before, damaging the part of her brainstem where movement and coordination are regulated. Although she was not completely paralyzed, her strength and coordination on both sides of her body were severely impaired, and she essentially had to learn how to utilize her muscles all over again. She could not walk or even transfer from bed to wheelchair, but as she made clear to me through her garbled words and asymmetric smile, she was determined to progress as far as was possible. The day she showed me her latest achievement—the ability to scratch her shoulder— she was proud and pleased, as the feat did represent a huge milestone. I was impressed.

Soon thereafter I was watching video highlights of a professional tennis tournament that had occurred earlier that day, and I marveled at the physical talent and prowess of the professional tennis players. At times they accomplished feats on the tennis court that seemed to defy the laws of physics. I was likewise impressed.

Now—admittedly making comparisons when none is required—which of those accomplishments could be considered more impressive?

The question clearly is not answerable, because the physical states and the contexts of their respective achievements were worlds apart. And to give each of them the credit they deserve, they all had worked as hard as they could to maximize whatever abilities they possessed. That being said, Shari faced an obstacle unknown to the tennis pros—almost complete muscular dysfunction—which presented huge physical and emotional challenges: Shari's weakness would tend to make anyone feel incompetent and discouraged, whereas the professionals enjoyed the exhilaration of physical prowess most of us cannot even imagine. I therefore believe Shari was at least their equal in accomplishment, if not their better, and I am not being sentimentally generous in my point of view. When you drill down to the core definition of what it means to make progress, it is not as important where we end up as where we end up *compared with where we started, given our inherent abilities.* I believe that is certainly the way God views the issue. Every parent who has been seen the first stumbling steps of a one-year-old child or, like me, has witnessed the snail-paced progress of his or her own disabled child, understands this truth.

When it comes to our inherent spirituality, all people are not created equal. I do not mean that God plays favorites, or that He unfairly blesses some of His children with special talent for spiritual devotion. In God's eyes there definitely are no favorites, but that does not mean we are created equal.

I witness this fact on a daily basis simply by observing my patients. Some have attention deficit disorder, or perhaps some form of intellectual developmental delay, or a psychiatric illness, making it hard for them to concentrate long enough to enter into contemplative prayer. Some have sleep apnea and tend to fall asleep whenever they become still. Many have chronic, often painful medical conditions that preclude prolonged prayer. Not a few of my patients were raised by horrible fathers, making it difficult to develop trust in a heavenly "Father." Others live paycheck to paycheck, sometimes working two jobs just to provide for their families, leaving virtually no time or energy for substantial prayer. I submit that every one of us has some form of handicap—big or small—that adversely affects our prayer life. Given these various handicaps, when speaking of our individual prayer lives, is it fair to expect that each of us must live up to the same standard of spiritual devotion?

This is not an idle question.

It is easy for us to become discouraged when, as we compare ourselves with certain Christians around us or with Saints throughout history, we conclude that our spirituality is second rate. But take heart—God is not so easily fooled! He knows in precise detail from what position we start our journey and exactly what personal limitations we bring to our prayer life, and He therefore also knows what is reasonable to expect of us. He is robustly practical ... and uncompromisingly fair. He sees the *relative* progress we make given our individual struggles. We are all, indeed, *not* created equal. But neither does God *treat* us equally—like any good father He takes our unique limitations into account.

So be at peace. Do not fret. And do not consider yourself a failure just because you struggle in your prayer life. He does not expect any more of you or of me than we can legitimately accomplish. Whether we spiritually are like Shari or more like a tennis professional, each of us can progress, *relative to our abilities and situations*, to the same extent. In that sense, God does not play favorites. We always should strive for deeper prayer—in fact, that should be one of our greatest goals in life, and we should never, ever use any of our limitations as an excuse for neglect of or laziness in prayer—but be happy that He is pleased with whatever steps you and I reasonably are able to take. Every one of those steps, if done with all the devotion and energy we can muster, is delightful to Him, and some of them might be just as worthy and treasured in God's eyes as marathons of prayer in the life of a cloistered Saint.

6

Your Head or Your Guts

Fundamental, transformational changes in a person's life are rarely accomplished through mere knowledge or mental choice. In my clinic, my patients already know what they should or should not do to be healthy (stop smoking, eat better, exercise, take their medications regularly, etc.). What is missing is not knowledge, but the galvanizing motivation that comes from their *bowels*, not from their brain. This truth was crystallized for me when I was working with a cancer specialist early in my medical training. One day I watched as this specialist told Brad, a young smoker, that he had terminal lung cancer. Brad was stunned. In his mind, he was still too young for that. As the cancer specialist gave him the bad news, I witnessed a rapid and physical change in Brad's face that can neither be described nor imitated—something in the eyes and the facial muscles. I was mesmerized.

For a moment there was total silence in the room. In his shirt pocket Brad happened to have a pack of cigarettes, which he wordlessly removed, studied for a few seconds, and then slowly and gently—with unnerving calm—placed on a side table. He looked back up at the cancer specialist with a glazed expression.

He never picked up a cigarette again. Later he told me he never even had the desire to do so. His smoking habit had been instantly cured, because the news of his cancer hit him in his guts, where it counts, not in his head, where he always knew he should quit. Two months later, cigarette free, Brad told me he felt great, healthier than he had felt in years. He could taste his food, smell the flowers, and felt "clean," and he wondered why he had not quit before. Three months later he died.

Brad's problem was never lack of knowledge. The same is true for you and me. We know, in our minds, that worldly ambitions and pleasures will never bring us fulfillment. We know that we should make our faith *the* priority, carving time out of our daily rat race for devotion. But the consequences of our spiritual sloth have not yet hit us in the guts where it counts—they remain in our brains. One day those consequences might hit home, either because of some calamity in our lives, or when we are on our deathbed (if we are blessed to face our death still fully conscious), or perhaps at some other time. At that point we will shed our superficial perspectives like my patient shed his cigarettes. But why do we wait until then? That is gambling with our faith, in that we might never have the opportunity to change.

And yet! And yet!

In legitimate defense of our weaknesses, we do have to admit that it *is* hard for us to make fundamental changes in our Christian devotion simply by telling ourselves to do so. "I know I should love God more" is rarely enough to make us Saints. I wish it were enough (it should be!), but we humans are creatures of habit and are typically slow to change. The gut-level, galvanizing changes in our devotional lives that I describe in this book—although they do require us to consciously *choose*—often happen "to us" as much as "because of us." We can work at it, as we should with every ounce of our energy, but we typically cannot force the change to occur with our minds alone, any more than we can force ourselves to feel God's presence just by intellectual choice. As an example, stop reading this book for thirty seconds and try to make yourself "be spiritual."

The answer to this difficulty, as you might have surmised, is to let God hit us in the guts. He does love to do so. Gut-level change is a gift of God, an outreach of His grace, even when the cause of this change is painful. And although you and I cannot *make* such a change happen, we can place ourselves into a situation in which we can *allow* it to happen.

There is no better place to start than in prayer.

But it must be prayer that focuses on *relationship* rather than on mere duty, or tradition, or our requests, or the like. If you engage in prayer in the way I describe in this book, I believe you will be deeply moved and motivated at some point. Do not expect some earth-shattering revelation. Expect His *presence*. This might take time—sometimes more time than we would like, because God often has to work in our hearts first during our daily lives to prepare us to hear and receive Him to our deepest advantage—but I believe it will occur. You cannot stand next to a sizzling fireplace without feeling the warmth, and the closer you stand, the warmer you get. Likewise, you cannot dwell consistently in the presence of God without sensing His presence at some point. That experience is galvanizing, and the more you dwell, the more galvanized you become. This is the perfect antidote to indifference.

In the end, only God's presence can hit us hard enough to overcome our spiritual inertia. Our part is in wanting that to happen ...

... and in putting ourselves in the position to have it so.

7

God's Clinic

"I'm fine!"

Sheila's eyes locked onto mine. Her tone was stern—almost a shout—and her words were accompanied by a furrowed brow, no hint of a smile, and a finger pointed threateningly at my face. She let the words hang in the air for a moment.

I had just walked into the clinic room smiling, her chart in my hand, and had greeted her warmly. There was no return smile and no amicable greeting—just two words and a look that could melt iron.

Sheila, in actuality, was a very pleasant forty-two-year-old woman, not prone to complaint, and she had always been delightful during her prior appointments. It had been a few years since her last health evaluation, so she was a bit behind on her medical care. It was good to see her again.

Taken aback by her "greeting," I froze midstride and looked at her more closely, my smile replaced by a surprised expression. Her finger was still pointed at me, but at the corners of her mouth I could see the beginnings of a shy grin. With a softer tone of voice she clarified her contention. "I'm fine," she repeated calmly. "I'm healthy, and there is nothing wrong with me. I am *only* here to have you look at two moles on my right thigh to make sure they are not cancer. *Nothing else!* Everything else is fine." Thereupon she pulled up her skirt a little so I could see two slightly darkened moles on her right anterior thigh. Having seen thousands of such lesions, I immediately recognized them as harmless, and I told her so.

Reassured, she thanked me and made preliminary steps to leave. Kindly, with a playful smile on my face but also with purpose, I stopped her premature exit, mentioning that I had not seen her in a while. She threw her head back and groaned toward the ceiling, "I *knew* you were going to say that!" She chuckled a little, knowing she had been caught. I also chuckled, now understanding why she had started the visit with her emphatic, "I'm fine!"

Glancing through her chart, I noted that, among other overdue issues such as immunizations, lab tests, and a general medical evaluation, she had not had her annual female physical for several years. Clinic schedules typically are too tight to fit in such a complete exam at the last moment, but this day I had some extra time. I also knew that she might not come back if I did not do the exam now, so I politely offered to do so. She groaned again, but with humor. She then admitted that she had been putting it off and knew it had to be done, so she agreed with little reluctance. She said she "just wanted to get it over with."

The exam was performed ... but Sheila was not fine. I found a mass where the right ovary was situated, and she had signs of silent intestinal bleeding. Given her age, there was a strong possibility that either or both of these issues could represent cancer. As I always do with my patients, I discussed my findings with her, detailing their possible meanings. I ordered multiple lab tests and a pelvic ultrasound, and I referred her for a colonoscopy. There was no further humor during the visit, except for her final comment, "Well, so much for telling you I'm fine!"

This story ends well, in that her right ovarian "mass" turned out to be a benign ovarian cyst that later resolved, and her silent bleeding was not from cancer—the intestinal workup was negative. Consequently, several visits and weeks later, we laughed about the whole affair, mutually relieved and happy that all was okay. But it might not have been so.

In the beginning Sheila's problem—if you can even consider it a problem—was that she was in my clinic in the first place. If you want nothing to be wrong, then a physician's office is not the place to be! We are a nosy, probing profession, trained to dig into areas of patients' lives that they prefer to keep private. Our goal is health, not comfort. No patient can conclude *before the fact* that a physician will provide a clean bill of health at the end. In truth, we physicians, as well as our patients, want everything to be fine, but if something is wrong, it is our duty and commitment to sniff it out as early as possible, even if that is not to the patient's liking.

Prayer is like that. When we come before the Lord, we are in the presence of the Great Physician. How often do we start our prayers with the claim "I'm fine!" even if we do not consciously say or think that? We present our concerns and requests to Him, as Sheila pointed out her two moles to me, and then we consider the visit over. Our business with God is accomplished. But the Great Physician is not done with us so easily! As hard as it might be to imagine, is it possible that you and I are somewhat overdue for His expert examination of our spiritual health? Heaven forbid! Me? But I feel fine. No major sins going on here! I even feel close to God.

I am not saying that our Lord is waiting to spoil our joyful mood or sense of holiness. After all, I often find my patients to be healthy, and it is a joyful thing to tell them so and to share in that news. God does the same. "Well done" are two of my favorite words of Jesus. What I *am* saying is that you and I can have areas of spiritual ill health that creep in silently, like Sheila's problems. These issues are so much easier to deal with when small and caught early … but *only* if we let the Great Physician be a "great physician." We must submit to His examination and treatment. *Listen* during prayer. If we are healthy, then we can rejoice in that fact. But while in His presence, we also should reflect on areas of our lives that are problematic, to see how we might be part of the problem—exercising the indispensable muscle of humility. Do we have areas of spiritual or emotional pain that we are ignoring because they feel better left untouched? Do we not want to accept God's "prescriptions" because His medicine does not always taste good?

It is no good trying to avoid His care. As a human physician, I have limits. Sheila, once out of my clinic, would have been out of my reach if she had decided to delay her exam even more. In contrast, we are never out of the Great Physician's reach … unless we insist on being so. He will—for *our* sake—hound us back to Him in order to promote healing. Ever since the fall of Adam and Eve, that has been His nonstop goal. During our prayer times, would it not be easier for us to start our visit in His heavenly clinic with the phrase, "I think I'm fine, but could You make sure?"

In response, our Physician does not always answer immediately. He can, of course, do so. But more often He prefers to lead us into situations in which our flaws become visible to us, so that we can let Him work on them. Personally, I think we learn best that way, and that is one of the reasons why, I believe, we typically have *more* struggles in life as our prayer life deepens—they are God's "diagnostic tests" that reveal to us our spiritual illnesses. We need those struggles so that we can grow in our faith, and God always wants us to grow. Furthermore, as our faith grows stronger and our devotional life deepens, God can reveal ever bigger character flaws to us because we are more spiritually and emotionally mature, capable of facing them with humility and with hope.

The quintessential Scriptural example of this process is chapter 4 in the gospel of Mark: Teaching His disciples, Jesus first gives several parables about the "Word of God" and how His disciples should respond to that Word when they hear it. At the end of the chapter, Jesus lets His disciples try out what they have just learned by getting into a boat with them and saying, "Let us go to the other side." Jesus—as God—is sowing the Word, and His sentence implies, "We *will* get to the other side," not "I *hope we make it* to the other side." How do the disciples respond to the Word? The weather turns sour, and they panic, because trust is not yet strong in their hearts. So much for all of the lessons learned from the parables of Mark 4! Jesus scolds their lack of faith, not because He is angry with them, but because He needed to point out to them their imperfection. How else would they grow?

It is often uncomfortable to undergo an examination by the Great Physician, just as it was for Sheila and for the disciples in Mark 4—there are unwelcome tests, the feeling of vulnerability, hearing news we do not want to hear, seeing imperfections or weaknesses in ourselves that we do not want to see. I know of no one who enjoys such things. But our Lord is the consummate physician, the best of the trade, and we could never be in better hands. If we submit to His workup, we are destined for spiritual health and happiness beyond all description. His clinic is always open.

Are we willing to keep our appointments?

8

Fully Aware

The greatest reward I receive for my work as a physician is a heartfelt thanks. There is no substitute for that grateful look in my patients' eyes or in that appreciative tone of voice—or in the eyes or voice of their family members—when I help them in their time of need. It makes my profession thoroughly worthwhile. But the depth of my patients' appreciation is directly proportional to how aware they are of their need, of their illness, and of their inability to cope or survive without my intervention. Patients whose own lives or whose family members' lives I have saved are the most grateful, especially those who were critically ill and on the brink of death, or those whose lives had lost hope and direction. Their words never quite express what their eyes and tone of voice convey when they thank me.

Prayer should be like that. The degree to which I am grateful for God's graces is directly proportional to how clearly I see my need. My most joyful prayers are wonderful experiences that can bring me to tears, but without exception, *every one* of those particular prayers—as joyful and exhilarating as they might be—are characterized by an honest self-understanding of my shortcomings. That recognition of my need does not in any way take away from the joy of the prayer. Rather, this self-understanding complements and completes my joy. These prayers would have been less wonderful without that understanding. When I pray, I want to be *fully aware* of my faults, as well as of my strengths, because genuine joy is always based on truth, not on denial—the former ushers in love of God and appreciation of His mercies; the latter brings only spiritual blindness.

9

Mirrors

Susan, an attractive girl in her midteens, had trouble maintaining eye contact with me. We recently had moved our medical practice to a new clinic building, and the exam rooms were still being organized and supplied with the usual supplies and necessities. We consider it a common courtesy for patients to have access to a mirror somewhere in each clinic room, usually inside an accessible cabinet, for purposes of reorganizing their attire after exams, tending to disheveled hair, etc. This particular morning I was talking with Susan, who was sitting on the exam table in front of me, about potentially serious physical symptoms she had been experiencing.

As is often the case for her age group, she had a precisely arranged hairstyle and a generous amount of facial makeup, and she was noticeably self-conscious. Unfortunately, the mirror for that clinic room had not yet been mounted inside the cabinet, and someone had left it leaning upright on the counter top, directly in Susan's line of sight if she looked sideways to her left. I was standing in front of her, trying to discuss her symptoms, but the temptation of the mirror was too much. Every five seconds or so—interspersed with my questions—Susan would steal a glance to her left to check on her appearance. With each look at herself in the mirror, she would smooth out a wrinkle in her shirt, correct a small defect in her makeup, or adjust her hairdo by putting a stray hair back into perfect alignment.

It was impossibly distracting, and her self-absorption—although understandable and certainly forgivable given her age—made my evaluation impossible. In terms of her health, she was in significant need. Help was standing right in front of her, but she could not avail herself of that help. For any hope of a diagnosis and a cure, Susan would have to take her eyes off of herself and concentrate on me. She would have to see her physical symptoms through my eyes as I guided her by my questions, drawing out insights that she formerly could not have recognized. Otherwise what she was experiencing would remain a confusing set of symptoms beyond her ability to understand. In short, she would need to stop looking at her appearance in that mirror on the counter and instead let *me* be her mirror.

She was not able to do so.

The mirror was too much for her. Gazing at herself repeatedly, she could not follow my train of thought, nor could she think clearly enough about her physical symptoms to answer my questions. I did not want to hurt her feelings by moving the mirror, so I subtly moved around the room in small stages to her right side until she could no longer turn to see the mirror. Only then did we make progress.

Prayer can be like that. You and I cannot claim any better insight into most of our spiritual maladies than young Susan could claim about her medical problem. We need *God's* insight to make sense of our deepest spiritual needs. If our attention during prayer is constantly diverted to the superficial aspects of our lives, we are unable to let God accomplish any meaningful work in our innermost hearts, where the true spiritual battles take place. During prayer we must take our spiritual eyes off of ourselves and look straight at God. After all, it is only in yielding to *His* examination of our heart, in viewing ourselves through *His eyes,* that we can see ourselves clearly.

He is a very effective mirror.

10

Burst Prayers

The difference was subtle, but it made all the difference.

Angelica was describing her situation, and it did not sound pleasant. Under lots of stress from work and from home, she was having trouble coping. Hers was a long story, describing a truly difficult set of circumstances in which she did not have many options, and our discussion took quite a while. Her two energetic young children were in the clinic room with us, alternately trying to keep themselves busy with coloring books and trying to get attention from their mother. The first goal was easy; the latter goal not so. No matter their tactics, whether simply approaching their mom to lean against her thigh, trying to ask her a question, or attempting to show her their latest coloring book "masterpiece," they were unable to elicit any kind of acknowledgment from her. She was remarkably tolerant of their attempted interruptions, not showing any irritation or rebuffing them outright, but she simply did not respond. Angelica was too absorbed in her thoughts, too caught up in her legitimately difficult story, so she unconsciously ignored the children. Behind the children's eyes there was a subtle but undeniable look of pain and of longing. When there was a sufficiently long break in our discussion such that she was not absorbed in her story, Angelica was able to redirect her focus to her children. At those times she was responsive and wonderfully encouraging to them—she was, at heart, a very devoted and kind young mother who wanted nothing but the best for her children. However, because of the intensity of her story as she talked with me, those breaks were few and far between, so the children spent most of the time looking and feeling relatively unnoticed. You could describe their contact time as somewhat "compartmentalized": this is time to focus on you, and this is time to focus on me—with a relatively sharp distinction between the two. I have known Angelica since she was young, and I have cared for her children since they were born, and although the above description is how she always interacted with her children when she was in my clinic, you will have to trust me when I say that Angelica was a very loving person and a devoted mother. At the moment, though, the children could not see it.

Victoria handled things differently. Like Angelica, she also had a stressful life and young children. Her story was no less difficult as she related it to me during her appointment. Her children, also given the coloring books to keep them happily distracted, would, like Angelica's children, intermittently interrupt their mother. However, unlike Angelica, Victoria would stop her discussion at an appropriate moment, give a brief word or two of encouragement or answer a simple question, and then resume our discussion. Never lengthy, these motherly interactions nevertheless frequently interrupted our conversation, but they never detracted from either Victoria's or my goals during the visit. In contrast to Angelica's children, Victoria's children had a look of peace and confidence. They exhibited no emotional strain in their voice or gaze, and they did not portray any longing for intimate relationship that had been denied them. Their interaction with their mother was *not* compartmentalized. As small as the differences were between Angelica's and Victoria's behavior, there was an enormous contrast between the children. What was missing from Angelica's interactions were the frequent, brief expressions of affection and connection that are essential to a child's happiness.

One of the best—if not outright *the* best—books ever written on the subject of devotion is *Introduction to the Devout Life*, by St. Francis de Sales. I cannot recommend it highly enough. In that book St. Francis recommends "ejaculatory prayers," by which he means those short prayers of a few words that spontaneously arise in our hearts all day long in response to small, everyday experiences. For reasons of the modern use of vocabulary—especially in my medical context—I prefer not to use that term, but rather to call these prayers "burst prayers," as they burst forth from our hearts in response to small events.[6] These brief prayers should pepper our day, whatever the context. Examples include: You see a beautiful sunset, and you pray, "Make my heart that beautiful." Seeing someone perform an act of kindness prompts you to pray that you might do the same. Conversely, witnessing an act of unkindness prompts you to ask God to help you never be unkind. You hear a siren in the distance, and you pray, "Lord, be with whomever is in acute need right now." This list of examples could be endless. St. Francis goes so far as to say that our other, longer prayers cannot be fruitful if we do not actively engage in those short burst prayers throughout the day.

Angelica and Victoria beautifully demonstrate the validity of St. Francis's point. Both mothers were equally supportive and encouraging when they had the opportunity to fully focus on

---

[6] Whatever anyone chooses to call these prayers, this idea originates wholly from St. Francis, not from me.

their respective children, but only Victoria was able to include those frequent, brief, and simple "bursts" of communication with her children that peppered our conversation during her clinic visit. So her relationship with her children—who were always in touch with their mother's attentive presence, never feeling neglected or unimportant—was stronger for it. Although the comparison between these two families and our relationship with God has obvious limitations,[7] the key point is still valid: The depth of devotion, the quality of relationship we have with God, and the degree to which we sense His presence during our daily lives are all directly proportional to the amount of burst prayers we utter throughout the day. It is not God, of course, but we who need those prayers. And St. Francis is right: without them our longer prayers are less fruitful.

God is always at hand, wanting to fill us and striving to be our constant companion. He desires so much more time with us than just our "devotional time" of prayer at the beginning or end of the day. Our prayer lives should never be compartmentalized, lest we find ourselves spiritually drifting away from His presence. St. Francis's view is that such spiritual drifting is inevitable without burst prayers. You and I need that constant loving connection in order to grow up spiritually happy and fulfilled as His children, full of peace, confidence, and love for Him. God wants our entire day to be filled with His presence. Indeed, there should be no clear distinction between our dedicated prayer time and our daily activity time—they both should be one and the same, with

---

[7] Not least of which is that Angelica and Victoria, who are the parents, are the ones who are doing the compartmentalizing, whereas in our lives it is you and I (represented by the children in the story) who do so. We can rest assured that God never compartmentalizes. My point in this metaphorical story is simply to convey how compartmentalization of loving interaction—which, in the context of this book, means prayer—negatively affects the quality of relationship.

us always aware of God's presence, talking with Him all day long. He is, after all, intimately involved in every experience we have, big or small, and He is, like any good parent, trying to teach us lessons about life at every opportunity.

He also happens to be someone well worth talking to.

11

Health versus Stealth

The cross-country skiing trip to the mountains with his colleagues had been fantastic. Stan, a fellow physician and close friend, was wonderfully content. At sixty-five years old he had been cross-country skiing in the mountains with some other physicians in our medical group, and despite the eight thousand–foot altitude, he had kept up with colleagues less than half his age. When he related to me the exhilaration of his feat, he was not boasting. I remember his countenance well: He was simply and humbly appreciating the joy of good health at his age. Two weeks later at sea level, in a moment of relaxation with no strain on his heart, he suffered his heart attack. Fortunately for him it was not a big one, but it was a heart attack nonetheless. He later marveled at the irony of it all: when under stress his heart did fine, but when at rest his heart suffered damage. When feeling most healthy while skiing, his heart's illness was stealthily moving forward without his knowledge.

Recently I have had to inform several relatively young patients—who were hard working, physically fit, and feeling well—that they had advanced and possibly terminal cancer. The news changed their entire worldview in an instant: one moment enjoying health, and the next moment facing the possibility of impending death.

Good health is a priority for almost everyone, although to varying degrees. The most proactive among us—whether from the appropriate desire to be healthy, or from a fear of dying—will exercise religiously, take a multitude of health supplements, avoid bad habits, eat a meticulously healthy diet, never "cheat" on their choice of foods, or do anything else that might lead to a longer and better life. Others of us take more modest strides to be healthy, and some of us do not make any effort at all.

But even the most dedicated health-seeking patients are vulnerable to the stealth of disease. None of us is exempt. Cancer starts with a single microscopic cell that loses inhibition and won't stop reproducing. Who among us can be certain that one of our cells is not making that transition right now while we are reading this sentence? The departure from health usually starts that way: with absolute stealth.

Does that make us anxious? Or worse? The possibility of developing cancer understandably should give us pause and concern. But outright *fear*? Are we still in that much bondage to our fear of death?

We all know that we cannot eliminate our vulnerability to disease. What is happening in our bodies right now is a mystery, even if we happen to be the smartest physician on the planet, a master of the trade. Although none of us likes that fact—it threatens our need to feel like we are in control—it is important never to hide from that truth. In my life it keeps me spiritually honest: I am, in truth, *never* in control. The control I crave during my weaker moments is a myth, even when I assume that I have it. I know that I will never be able to eliminate my vulnerability to disease and death, and reflecting upon the fact that one of my cells or blood vessels could betray me at any moment, I realize that even mundane, day-to-day life *forces me to trust*: Trust that my life is cared for by the Lord. Trust that He knows what is best not just *for* me at this moment, but also what is best that should happen *to* me in my place in human history. After all, the greatest importance of my life is not in how *I* experience it but in how my life—and death—contribute to His plan for human history and for His other children.

I do not dwell on and wallow in the truth that I could develop cancer at any moment, as that would be morbid and self-absorbed. But I am thankful that I cannot hide from my vulnerability—my experiences with my patients do not let me. What I see in them could happen equally easily to me, so I am spurred to greater trust and to a greater desire not to waste my life in frivolous pursuits. In the end, none of us has any other option than to trust: trust in the myth of our own control while living in denial of our vulnerability, or trust that the God who would never be unjust will take care of us. As Christians, those are the only two options available. One way or another I try to remember that fact during every dedicated time of prayer. It keeps me honest ...

... and trusting.

12

Sorrow

"Don't you *dare* die! Don't you even think about it!"

She was screaming at her son. Her son—now sedated and on a ventilator—who could no longer hear her. He had waited too long to seek medical care, and it was now too late. His mother's voice echoed through the entire emergency room. "If you die, I'll kill you!" Desperate, angry, and grieving at the same time, unable to come to grips with the abrupt and tragic turn of events that was partly due to her son's stubbornness, she was screaming the absurd—because the context was absurd, more nightmare than reality to her. Her voice had that indescribable tone that, once heard, is not easily forgotten. It haunts a physician's memory. Her son, twenty years old and otherwise in good health, was dying of an asthmatic attack that got out of control because of his procrastination, and medically speaking, it was already too late. He was dying. The day before he had been relatively fine, with a future ahead of him, but now he was slipping away from his mother's care. It was incomprehensible to her. The quality of her voice was not simply panicked. These situations take on a nightmarish quality, a sense of the surreal, a feeling that "this cannot be happening!" So the voice takes on the hue of a nightmarish scream, of the participation in a horror from which one is supposed to wake up any moment—but cannot.

Very recently, in a different experience, I stood with our close friends at the burial of their son, a victim of cancer at the age of four years old. He was their only child together. He was also our godson. We were all saying our final good-byes, and during the service the parents' sobs did not stop. At the conclusion of the service, his mother was glued to the side of the grave, incapable of leaving her son behind, and when, with the guidance and encouraging arms of those around her, she negotiated that final turning away, her facial expression defied description.

We do not know why we suffer such losses. There is a mystery and there are ultimate purposes to these tragedies far beyond our individual or collective wisdom. My goal in writing this chapter is not to offer an explanation for this mystery, but rather to reflect on the God with whom we grieve.

For parents such as those I mention above, superficial responses during the acute grieving process provide no consolation. I have heard Christians offer such glib words as, "Don't be so sad. Take heart. Your child is in heaven now. He is in a better place. Be happy for him." True as the facts of the deceased child's resting place might be, in my opinion these unsolicited phrases are cruel in the midst of acute grief. Such words delegitimize and scold a parent's heartache, implying that the agony should not be so agonizing. No one in his right mind should accuse bereaved parents that their grief is inappropriately intense. We Christians do not grieve as those "with no hope," but our grief can still feel infinitely deep. Christians have hope *not* because our grief should seem less than infinitely deep but because God is deeper than infinity. He will catch us as our hearts emotionally fall and reunite us with our loved ones in the end, but He never rebukes our cries of pain. You only need look at the life of Jesus to see that.

I sometimes am asked what I say to my patients at these times of intense suffering. The answer is easy: I say very little. Other than uttering a short phrase such as "I am so sorry" or "This is so hard" or "I miss Miguelito too," all I can do is give my patients a long bear hug and cry with them. And that is usually all they want or need. Words—unless specifically solicited by the patient—are usually more hindrance than help. In our culture that seeks to avoid pain above all else, there is a temptation to try and "fix it" with just the right words of wisdom or encouragement. Grieving patients do not need to be fixed. They need to be consoled and comforted. They require the compassionate presence of someone who is not afraid of suffering.

And God is the ultimate consoler.

"But," it is fair for even the most faithful believer to ask, "in what way does God console?" After all, during acute anguish it can feel like He is nowhere to be found, and our pain can overwhelm our prayers and make us question God's role in our loss. In our hurt and anger (a normal human response by which God, in my opinion, is not offended) do we cry out in our hearts, "Does God not care?! Is heaven, where God resides, immune to pain?" One can hardly criticize a grieving parent for raising such questions. In reality, God does console us. But—with due reverence to our Lord—I believe it is legitimate for a grieving parent to ask what kind of consolation God offers.

To answer that—although there are innumerable causes of grief that could be discussed, and although no form of grief should be considered by external observers as less important than any other—let me use the example of losing a child. And I will start by asking a question that should not need to be asked: Is intense grief over the loss of one's child ungodly? Does it represent a lack of faith in the goodness of God? Or does it recognize too little appreciation of the joys of heaven for the child? To state the obvious, of course not. In my view, the heartache of parents during such tragedies is not just understandable, it is *godly*. Such grief is not merely right and fitting, but I believe its absence would indicate great evil. And if such sorrow is godly, what does that therefore say about God, who is the source of all that is godly? Can a parent's grief somehow be found in God? Can there be true—not token—shared empathy and genuine sorrow in God's heart? Can heaven, where there is only pure joy, include heartache? With all my heart, I believe so.

Do we think God is unmoved when His children suffer loss? Is He untouched by the heartache of people whom He loves more than we do? When crying out to Him in pain, could we ever hear in return, "I am sorry, but I cannot feel your agony because I am so happy in heaven that your earthly sorrow does not touch me"? Unthinkable! His sorrow does not contain the fear, doubts, anger, loneliness, hopelessness, despair, and feelings of defeat that so often characterize human sorrow. His is a godly sorrow, full of hope and strength—a mystery, to be sure—but it is somehow true sorrow nonetheless. God empathetically and intimately *knows and has tasted pain* (look at Jesus) and understands our suffering. And that makes all the difference! My wife and I have lost a newborn child. Twice we were within a hair's breadth of losing two other daughters when they were young. And other tragedies of equal pain and far longer consequences have touched our family that do not bear telling. Many families have suffered far more than ours, but we have had our share. Earlier in my

Christian faith, when my prayer life was more intellectual and less founded in relationship, I found it difficult to pray through such crises. What is there to say when pain is beyond words? What is there to ask when I am too confounded, depressed, and afraid of the future to think clearly? Now that my prayer life has deepened, I am content simply to cry. In the whirlwind of heartache and confusion, my prayers are reduced to curling up in my Father's lap, sobbing or groaning, and saying very little. I do not experience any "spiritual high" or deep wisdom. I simply hurt, and I feel very discouraged. Yet at those moments, whether or not I feel Him emotionally, I know that He holds me and that He in some mysterious fashion *cries alongside me*, like I used to do when my daughters cried on my lap. Even though, after I let it all out, I am no closer to understanding life than before, I know that I am neither alone nor abandoned. I realize He has answers for what is happening, even if I do not, but my focus is not on getting those answers (He will give them to me when it is best). My outcries are not intellectual, or even theological—they are *visceral*: they hurt in my guts. So I pray from my guts. If I believed that my Father's response to such prayers was to scold me to have more faith or be more thankful, I do not think I would ever make it through. I am comforted that heavenly joy *embraces* my sorrow rather than condemns it.

Revelation 21:4 states that all suffering and pain will pass away at the end, but that end has not yet arrived. Thankfully, the promise of future deliverance from pain and sorrow—and more specifically the reunification with our loved ones—brings us our ultimate hope, and we can cling to that hope with confidence. In the meantime, we all experience deep pain here on earth at one point or another, sometimes even pain beyond all reckoning, and God feels it right along with us. Answers to "Why?!!" might not come during our lifetime, but consolation is always at hand.

Like any good parent, God eventually brings us through to a more positive place of peace and thanksgiving, and if we are able to understand, He will reveal to us the reasons for our loss. But those things come later and over time. In the midst of the heartache He does not preach to us or scold us, but rather He holds us, and He mourns with us.

I am comforted that I can pray to such a Father.

13

Well Done

Keisha was fussy. Tired, impatient, perhaps hungry—nine-month-old babies do not provide verbal summaries of their needs—she was not responding to her father's consolation during her well child visit. While I tried to pursue a line of questioning with her father about her health, Keisha wiggled and fussed in his arms, making it difficult for him to concentrate on my questions. A good father, he was patient with Keisha, but things were not going smoothly. It was tough to make much progress in my evaluation.

Then came Michael.

A mere two years older than his sister, it was unrealistic to expect him to help. Nevertheless, while happily playing with his toys in the corner of the room, he noticed Keisha's troubles, and leaving the comfort of his corner, he came over to his sister. By talking to her, caressing her face, and sharing the toy he brought from the corner, Michael tried to cheer her up. It worked! She started to giggle, her fussing stopped, and her father could once again focus on the health issues at hand. Young and inexperienced as he was, Michael was nevertheless marvelous.

At one point when the father and I paused in our conversation, Michael looked up, and his father looked down. For a moment their eyes connected: the father smiled at his son with pride and obvious delight; the son, recognizing and responding to that look on his father's face, beamed with his own pride and delight. The wordless interchange was brief but potent: an encyclopedia of meanings passed between the two in the blink of an eye.

We are all like Michael: young, simple, not very impressive or wise, but (I hope!) consistently trying to help where we can. All we can expect of ourselves is to aid those close at hand, doing whatever is feasible at the moment *if* we stay vigilant to the needs around us. Even the Mother Teresas of this world live their lives that way. The smallest of kindnesses count. Nothing escapes the Father's awareness, and our Father, far from being a distant and demanding taskmaster, *delights* in those small deeds of mercy. In essence, my life as a physician is nothing more than a string of such small works. In God's eyes every job, whether the world considers it glamorous or not, has the same importance and offers opportunities to serve others. Those opportunities take different forms—some obvious and others subtle—but they always are there.

We want to make our Father proud of us—not because we earn it, but because He, like any good father, delights in our efforts. Receiving a "well done" from Him is a reward beyond measure. Lord willing, our reception of God's loving pleasure will be fully realized when we see Him at our death, but even now we can get a taste of His delight. Personally, I long for that same look that Michael shared with his father, but from my Father in heaven. I receive it in my heart, not in my eyes, but it is His look nevertheless. It is a thrill that can enliven our prayers.

Look for it. All you have to do is steadfastly help those around you, and then gaze upward in prayer ...

... He *always* is gazing down at you.

14

Getting in Shape

Why is it that my patients who are in better physical shape seem to enjoy more benefit from exercise than my patients who are chronically deconditioned? One would think that the deconditioned patient stands to gain so much more from exercise. Ultimately that is true—but not initially. Those who first start to exercise have to struggle and work hard (mentally and physically) to maintain this new and healthy habit. And their initial rewards for this admirable new healthy activity are often sore muscles and fatigue, *not* the feeling of good health. I therefore always recommend starting out with minimal exercise, and I give a warning to increase the duration and intensity *slowly*. My usual message to the patient is, "Get in tone (i.e., get used to exercising) before you get in shape." Over time, as these patients become more physically conditioned, they have an easier and more enjoyable time maintaining their exercise regimen. Exercise—by doing it *daily*, even if only for a few minutes—thereby not only becomes a habit, but it also brings the *tangible experience* of good health. Tasting these rewards, the patients want more, so they exercise more consistently. In contrast to patients who are in a "negative downward spiral" of ill health, these exercising patients experience what is called a "positive upward cycle." They *become* healthier, and they also *feel* healthier, which fosters this newfound healthy lifestyle.

Prayer involves the same process. Why is it that Christians who pray consistently seem to get more out of their prayers? Is that fair? Or is fairness even the right question? Similar to being physically fit, being "spiritually fit" yields tangible rewards. The lack of heartfelt rewards during prayer in the believer who prays less can never be blamed on God for holding back His presence. It is not lack of knowledge or lack of pleasure that keeps a Christian from praying consistently. Getting in shape— physically or spiritually—takes an initial investment, and it usually does not feel rewarding in the beginning. The Christian who has gotten out of the habit of praying unavoidably must go through that first stage of getting back in shape. This stage is uncomfortable, as it takes place before the fruits of consistent prayer are once again realized.

The best advice is to start with minimal time and advance slowly. Regarding physical exercise, I tell my patients that *frequency is more important than duration.* Just five minutes of exercise five days a week (five times five) is better than ten minutes of exercise three days a week (ten times three), even though the latter involves more total time. I then tell my patients to increase the duration little by little, as their stamina allows. I would rather have my patients exercise five times five for the rest of their lives than increase the duration too quickly and burn out, thereby giving up exercise altogether. Besides, I have never had a patient exercise five days a week for five minutes and not eventually increase the exercise duration to ten minutes. Once in the habit of exercise, these patients enjoy the benefits of feeling healthier, so their motivation takes over. Prayer is similar. I therefore urge realism: Do not overextend yourself too quickly. Remember: frequency above duration. Develop the *habit* of prayer. You are in it for the long haul, so pace yourself like the long-distance runner, not the sprinter.

15

Style

If I had shown Max too much empathy, he probably would have walked out. If I had shown Danny too little, he might have done the same.

No surprise to anyone, my patients come to my clinic with an infinite variety of personalities. Some, like Max, are tough, straight talking, no-nonsense, and not "into their feelings." Others, like Danny, are sensitive, empathetic, vulnerable, and very much in tune with their emotions. Between these two extremes lie the rest of us. And we all, over the years, slide back and forth across that spectrum depending on a host of factors: our age, our prior experiences, our life circumstances at any particular time, our motives and goals, to list just a few. Sometimes we lean toward Max and sometimes toward Danny.

What Max and Danny had in common was that they both were confiding in me about symptoms of depression. Max was decidedly uncomfortable with the topic, and it was excruciatingly hard for him to bring up the issue in the first place, much less describe his emotions and discuss them with me. He was not accustomed to being vulnerable or to talking about his feelings, but to his credit, he did both. Danny, in contrast, was quite comfortable with the subject matter in general, but he was transparently anxious that I would think ill of him, that I might reject him or his feelings, or that he would appear weak. It was therefore just as hard for him to discuss his emotions with me as it was for Max, but for different reasons. To Danny's credit, his discomfort did not stop him either.

Max's and Danny's styles, which stemmed from their individual personalities, could not have been more different, but their needs and their goals were remarkably similar. My job, if I was to be successful as their physician, was not only to figure out how to best help them medically, but also to discern their styles of personal interaction—their unique personal conversational personalities—so that, as I asked questions, discussed their symptoms, and described treatment options, my help would be welcome and make them feel comfortable rather than be offensive, contrary to their personalities, and turn them off. My tone of voice, choice of words, choice of analogies, and body language were carefully tailored to suit each of their personal styles. With Max I was straightforward and matter-of-fact; with Danny I displayed a lot of empathy and expressed much encouragement. In the end, my message to each was fairly similar, but my approach decidedly was not. Had I interacted with either of them in any other way, things might not have gone well.

Over time, Max became more comfortable discussing his emotions with me, until eventually our conversations were surprisingly relaxed and comfortable without the awkward strain of that first visit, and we were able talk about his depression at surprising length. Likewise, Danny also ultimately developed more ease during our discussions, shedding his insecurity and gaining more confidence, displaying a sense of personal strength, value, and acceptance, such that I was able to be more forthright with him without fear of offense. Both men, in a sense, moved toward each other on the spectrum of communication styles such that, after a while, one could even say that their styles began to overlap, despite their polar personalities.

Prayer is no different. In keeping with our personalities, during the early stages of developing an active prayer life, each of us finds certain styles of prayer easier and more naturally suited to our character. I believe God has no problem with those differences. Too often—and I admit that the descriptions of prayer I use in this book may be contributing to this problem— prayer is portrayed in a singular way, namely as spending long periods of time on our knees with heads bowed and eyes closed. In reality, that style does not work for everyone initially ... or perhaps ever. Many Christians find such prayers fulfilling, but others pray best while on their feet working, while taking a walk, or in a myriad of other contexts. Some Christians pray for long periods of time all at once, while others tend to engage in burst prayers[8] all throughout the day. Personally, I do not think God really cares. The important issue is not so much the style of our prayers, but the heart and soul that go into them.

Because the growth in Max and Danny did not come easily at first, it was crucial at the start that they be allowed to interact with me in their comfort zone. It was *their* styles, not mine, that determined our interaction. So it is with many Christians who have a difficult time incorporating prayer into their lives. Perhaps this describes you. There is a desire to pray more, but your personal style does not readily fit with the "long time on your

---

[8] See the chapter on burst prayers.

knees" type of prayer. In my view, that is just fine. Your Father in heaven is a far better Physician than I, and if I—with my human limitations—am able to adjust my interaction to suit the needs of my patients, how much better can He do the same for you? If you are one of those Christians who is struggling to bring prayer back into your life, feel free in the beginning to approach Him in the way you feel most comfortable. He gladly will meet you there.

Three factors allowed Max and Danny to grow so much: both men had the courage to admit their need to me in the first place; they were allowed in the beginning to talk through their struggles in their own comfortable styles; and they had sufficient commitment to their health that they persevered in their pursuit of healing. As their lives progressed and improved, their styles matured and broadened. Similarly, if you begin to pray in the style you feel most comfortable, then over time, as you persevere in that prayer, you will naturally start to enjoy other styles of prayer. Do not make the mistake of putting off prayer until you "have enough time" for lengthy quiet times, as that might not happen for much or most of your life. Also do not make the mistake of thinking that there is only one way to pray—there are, in truth, many.

Just do not procrastinate!

In the beginning, choose your favorite style, and do not overdo it in terms of time commitment. I believe this is one of those situations in which God happily tells you—in the most positive sense of the words—to "suit yourself!" As time passes, your love of God and your sense of His presence will grow, and you will love the joy of longer and more varied prayer ... *if* you do with God what Max and Danny did with me.

Start somewhere ... your spiritual life depends on it.

16

Constant Prayer?[9]

When I was younger in my faith the phrase "be in constant prayer" confused me. How, if we are supposed to focus on what we are doing, can we be constantly praying? Years ago (I believe it was during my medical training, but I honestly cannot be sure) I remember a visiting pastor telling our congregation a true story about his own life. One day in high school he decided that he wanted to be in constant prayer, and so, to his great credit, with a genuine and sincere heart, he put that desire into practice. During every part of his life he talked with his Lord. In keeping with his devotion, that weekend, while playing as a front lineman for his school's football team, he was determined to pray throughout the entire game.

Of course, as simple logic and basic brain physiology would dictate, his nonstop focus on prayer required that he devote a section of his brain to that prayer, preventing that same section of his brain from concentrating on anything else—such as on the football game. It therefore should come as no surprise that

---

[9] I need to clarify that this story does not come specifically from my patients but rather from a Sunday sermon I heard during my medical training. I have forgotten the name of the pastor.

during one particular play, with an important part of his brain occupied with his prayer, he got mixed up about the plan. The football was to be handed off to the running back who would run to the left, with the various linemen (including the pastor) running to the left in front to clear a path for that running back. The pastor's position on the team was as the linemen on the farthest *left* side of the lineup, so not only would he be part of the first line of attack, but he would be leading the charge.

As the play began and the entire team ran to the left, the pastor—due to his divided and distracted mind—bolted in joyful prayer and with all his might to the right—straight into his teammates! Hallelujah! Crashing headlong into all of his unsuspecting fellow linemen, he knocked them down in one fell swoop, leaving the ball carrier alone to face the opposing players. Ahhh, such prayerfully rapturous joy ...

Alas, it is difficult to maintain spiritual fervor when your teammates glare at you, your coach screams your idiocy, and everyone in the stands is laughing uproariously. So much for constant prayer!

This true example is a rather humorous and harmless one, but imagine a scenario in which your physician makes the same mistake while caring for one of your critically ill family members during a medical emergency. Such an experience would not be humorous; it would be a nightmare. The pastor's error was not in his desire to pray unceasingly, but in his misunderstanding of prayer as conversation, as communication.[10]

---

[10] To his credit, the pastor likewise learned this lesson, which is why he told the story to us in the first place.

To oversimplify for purposes of clarification, prayer primarily is basking in God's presence, whether in conversation or in silence, just as courtship with my wife many years ago could involve words or simply could be basking in the joy of each other's company. I try to be in constant prayer today not by babbling nonstop to God in constant conversation—although conversation is an important part of prayer—but by having His heart close to mine, whether or not I am consciously concentrating on Him. As a Christian's prayer life deepens, the line between "praying" and "just living our day-to-day lives" becomes progressively blurred until it disappears altogether, *not* because God is forgotten at any time, but because He saturates the Christian's every moment. Although I have not yet come close to achieving that perfect blend, happily I am getting closer as I grow in faith. So now when I am involved in a medical crisis, as happened last week in the hospital during my patient's cardiac arrest, I am 100 percent focused on the task at hand, but with a comfort that God is working right along with me.

17

Change?

Lifestyle is the most difficult thing for a physician to change in a patient's life. Yet a healthy lifestyle is the cornerstone of good health. Each day a patient's lifestyle choices will affect his health, for better or for worse. In the same way, the Christian life is not static. It is dynamic, living, ever-changing, and ever-growing—or ever-shrinking. You are never sitting still in your spiritual life. You work toward deeper faith, or you drift toward shallower. Stagnation never occurs for any significant length of time.

This is true of prayer as much or more than of any other aspect of the Christian life. If you yield to God in prayer, *He changes you* for the better. If you ignore or resist Him, then *you change you* for the worse. Although it is naïve to assume that every prayer will be life-changing and emotionally moving (everyone's prayers, including my own, can feel dry), overall your prayers should make a difference. If in your prayers you meet God, then you cannot remain the same person. He changes you. He deepens your devotion—slowly, but surely. If this is not happening for you, then it is time to take action: seek instruction, get support among fellow believers, and pursue a different approach to prayer.

Your prayers should change you, or you should change your prayers.

18

The Most Frightening Verse

She looked decent and upstanding. Her medical chart said otherwise.

I was in the emergency room at my training hospital talking with a patient who was grimacing in apparent pain. Her husband was at the bedside, leaning toward her over the bedrails, holding her hand, concerned and entirely convinced by her story while she complained of abdominal pain and asked for pain medications. Her chart was very thick—my arms as well as my eyes told me that—thick with repetitive and well-documented incidences of manipulative narcotic-seeking behavior for a myriad of painful conditions, some of which were "severe abdominal pain." Such patients are among the most difficult to treat, as pain has no objective measure. If the patient is clever and a good actor, it can be tough for a physician to tell if the pain is real, imagined, or faked.

And yet these patients, like everyone else, can develop serious illnesses that must be compassionately treated. How to sort out truth from lie, the real need for pain medications from narcotic-seeking behavior, is extremely difficult, both emotionally and intellectually. Making it even more grueling for the physician, the personalities of entrenched drug-seeking patients can be quite taxing—there is a personal chemistry that is hard to define but is tough on a medical provider's nerves, forcing a conscientious doctor to expend an enormous amount of energy trying to be fair and accurate in the medical assessment.

After glancing through the patient's chart, I groaned inwardly. It was the afternoon near the end of a very long and stressful thirty-six-hour shift that had started the day before and had continued all night, and I was exhausted. Training in a hospital where there were many drug-seeking patients, I was now facing an expert in the art, and I barely had the energy to cope. I could not carelessly dismiss her complaints, as she might have a serious illness in her abdomen, but her pattern of behavior was clear as glass: get narcotics through any means possible. *Groan!*

I had been trained—in my medical school and residency as well as in church—to treat all of my patients with dignity, giving them the benefit of the doubt before coming to any premature conclusions. Therefore, with much effort and self-control, I remained respectful and treated her like any other patient. I began the usual series of questions to diagnose her abdominal "ailment." After a short time I noticed an ER nurse quietly slip into the exam room and approach me from the side opposite the patient and her husband. Asking out loud some token question that would justify her interruption, the nurse slipped me a new medical chart while taking away the bulky chart I was holding. She was good—the patient and her husband never noticed a thing. With an embarrassed smile, she silently signaled that I initially had been given the wrong patient's chart![11] I glanced

---

[11] This incident happened early in my training, and I was exhausted at the time, so I made the mistake of not verifying this patient's identity *before*

down. The medical record I now held was thin, lightweight, and described an upstanding young woman with no history of drug-seeking behavior.

I almost lost it.

Exhausted, a few minutes earlier I had come frighteningly close to maligning this innocent, suffering woman—not to mention her supportive husband, whom I had considered blind, duped, and codependent—with a disrespectful tone if not outright cynical words. And all would have been due to false information that had seemed irrefutably true at the time. I uttered an instant prayer of thanks that I had not listened to my prior disdain but had given her the benefit of the doubt. I turned to the patient once again, seeing her now in a clearer light, and continued the workup. Outwardly I appeared no different, as I had hidden my prior feelings. Inwardly I was shaken. Fortunately she and her husband never knew what had transpired. I thank God for that.

In my opinion, Matthew 7:2 is *by far* the most frightening verse in all of scripture. "For as you judge, so you will be judged ..." Have you ever stopped and contemplated what that verse *really* says? Do not make the mistake of interpreting the verse only in relation to our current lives. Yes, even here on earth often "what goes around comes around." But more importantly, one day you and I will die and confront the final judgment, and Jesus, with mercy and love—but also fairness and justice—will face us at our death. In His hands will be the "document" that you and I created with our day-to-day lives, detailing very clearly the rules of judgment *you and I wrote* by how we judged others when we were on earth. Did we tear people down in our hearts or in

---

starting the evaluation. I have never made that mistake again.

our actions because we were petty or jealous, or because we did not like them? Did we condescend because we viewed ourselves as superior in some way? Did we come to ill conclusions about someone's worth or status because we *thought* we know the truth about them, when in reality our information could have been misleading, incomplete, or simply false? We might not even have been at fault for receiving that false information, such as in my case above. But even in that scenario, *how did we treat the person?* With compassion or with condemnation? Wanting the best for them or the worst for them? What will it be like at our death when Jesus says, while leafing through our spiritual chart, "Okay, let's see how you prefer to handle things. Don't worry, we can do it your way ..." In the end, do you and I want to be judged using the standard of our own shortsightedness? This is one of the reasons I believe gossip is listed among the worst of sins (see Romans 1:29–30), because gossip not only corrodes the one who gossips and can hurt the reputation of the one gossiped about, but it also can lead susceptible hearers into false judgment of others. How easily we all become those "susceptible hearers"!

So how does the above relate to prayer? When on my knees, I need to approach the Holy of Holies without false judgment in my heart. When we enter into the presence of God during prayer, we are not approaching a doting, kindly, sentimental Grandfather figure. We come into the presence of a wise, insightful Father who effortlessly sees right through our facades. He is never fooled by any self-deception or self-justification we might put forth if we try to excuse or ignore our improper judgment of His other children. As a good Father, He also will never tolerate such an attitude in us ... nor would I want Him to do so. In fact, I eagerly *invite* Him to rid me of all such attitudes before I face Jesus at the end of my life. God's love is that of a true Father, in that He will do everything within His power, whatever the cost, to help us grow out of any improper judgmental tendencies we might possess—He does not want to raise spoiled or spiteful children. Whether He confronts us during our prayers or leads us into situations later on that clarify to us our error, He will not let us get away with judgmental attitudes that are harmful to ourselves and to others.

Lest I be misunderstood, I am not claiming we should avoid making judgments. We have a sacred responsibility to judge the things we see around us. How else could we navigate life, make correct choices, and protect ourselves and our loved ones from harm? But we should approach this need for judgment with extreme caution, as it is treacherous territory, full of slippery slopes. Speaking as a physician and as a father of four daughters, I believe it is permissible—even imperative—to discern between holy and unholy behavior in the people around us. But that discernment should always be done with humility, with patience, and with kindness to the persons involved, having their best outcome in mind. You and I will never know the entire story behind other people's lives, and our information is almost universally fallible. We essentially always get it wrong when we pass personal judgment on others—a fact that should give us great pause.

But even if—against all odds—our information is correct and we do get it right regarding someone else's behavior, we still need to be extremely careful. We too easily progress from correct *discernment* of people's actions to *condemnation* of the people themselves—a terrible misstep, even if only done in the privacy of our hearts. No, even for those who do not deserve it, our attitude should be one of love toward them, striving to serve them, not condemn them, praying for their best rather than for their worst, and acknowledging the embarrassing but strong probability that the flaws we see in their lives might also exist to some extent in our own. During our prayers, let us strive to let our Father rid us of errant judgment—at any cost—which is a *much* better alternative than having our attitudes come back to haunt us at our own personal reckoning.

19

Tracy

The look on Tracy's face is difficult to describe.

Eyes opened wide, eyebrows raised, lips pursed, with concern written all over her face, she was looking at me with part fear, part trust ... and mostly dread. I had just explained what needed to be done, but my report was not to her liking. Tracy had a large abscess in her private area that would have to be thoroughly cleansed, anesthetized as well as could be accomplished given its location, opened with a scalpel, probed and drained, and then packed with gauze—not a welcome procedure by any standards. But to ignore the abscess could be fatal, as such infections can dangerously spread. All the while, she would have to lie on the exam table in an embarrassing position, remain very still while not able to see what I was doing, ignore her instincts for privacy and protection, tolerate whatever pain was involved, and *completely* trust me to do what was necessary in a safe, efficient, and successful manner. For those few seconds of contemplation and internal debate, while I awaited her consent, Tracy's mind was in civil war—one side screaming to run, and the other urging calm and trust. Thankfully the trusting side won ... but it was not by a landslide.

After the procedure was over, Tracy's relief was enormous, and she was truly grateful. What she had dreaded was not as bad as she had feared, and although further healing remained, she already felt much better. Within the time span of a short medical procedure, her future had changed, escaping a downhill course that possibly could have destroyed her.

Prayer is no different. Although not always the case, there admittedly are times when God has to do to our souls what I did to Tracy's body. At those times I, for one, find myself in a mental civil war similar to Tracy's, as I do not relish God digging around in my private heart trying to fix things I would rather be left alone—no matter how important they might be to my spiritual health. Our temptation, when we know that we are not in the best state of grace with Him, is to avoid praying and showing up to His "clinic" at all. Or we might pray, but conveniently "not bring up the subject" with Him. As was true for Tracy physically, avoiding our spiritual maladies can be dangerously unhealthy, but there is no avoiding the fact that letting God do His work in us takes a lot of willpower and courage on our part.

Of course, several weeks later when Tracy was fully healed, she felt wonderful. In the end, the pleasure of restored physical health far outweighed the amount of suffering from the procedure. However, although this conclusion was obvious after the fact, it was not so clear before the procedure was started. Similarly, you and I will be overjoyed at the spiritual health we receive from God after His work in our hearts is done, but we will not feel that way beforehand. Nevertheless we should not delay. And we absolutely should neither ignore Him nor run away from Him completely. Our spiritual health is even more important than our physical health. Embarrassing, painful, and unwelcome though it may be, our Great Physician might be asking us right now to let Him do His work in us. As with Tracy, going through God's "procedures" is never as bad as we think it will be beforehand. We should let Him start.

Tremendous joy awaits us.

20

All That Trouble?

Trey was born with a moderate degree of physical and mental developmental delay, but at eighteen months of age, he also developed a malignant, incurable form of brain cancer located in his brainstem, in a narrow area just above the neck. It was a slow-growing type of cancer, but it grew relentlessly, making the final outcome inevitable. Trey would eventually die. From the time of diagnosis it took almost three years before he passed away, and all the while his parents, especially his mother who stayed home full time with him, took exceptional care of his many needs, even as his already significant disabilities slowly worsened from the pressure of the expanding tumor. I know this family well, and I can state categorically, without fear of contradiction, that either parent would have done anything to save Trey, their only child, including taking his place if that were possible. They were 100 percent devoted to him.

What if, instead of just one son, they had had five children? Or twenty children? Would the parents' devotion to Trey have been any different?

Would it have been *less*? In my view that could never happen. I cannot imagine a devoted parent loving a child less intensely just because there were other children in the home, as if an increase in number of siblings would make them more disposable. Alternatively, with more children in the home, would the parents' devotion to Trey have been *more*? That also would make no sense. Can anyone possibly be more than 100 percent devoted? No, in the end, the number of children is irrelevant. Whether one child or many, the parents would have been willing to sacrifice anything to save their child—or children.

In speaking of Jesus, C. S. Lewis writes, "He died not for men, but for each man. If each man had been the only man made, He would have done no less." [12] It is hard for us to wrap our minds around this truth, but it is true nonetheless: if you or I happened to be the only individual in all of history who chose to be saved, Jesus would have gone through the entire process of salvation for either one of us. Because of our fallen nature and the limitations of our human understanding, when we contemplate this truth, we typically are amazed that God would do such a thing, that He would go to all that trouble just for you or for me. But is such amazement proper?

Should we marvel at this truth? Yes. Be humbled and thankful for it down to our bones? No question. Be awed by it? Absolutely! But be in any way amazed by it like I describe above?

No.

I believe that any sense of amazement—or you could as easily use the word *surprise*—would be in error, but not primarily

[12] The recognition of this truth long preceded Lewis, but he has a remarkably talented way of expressing it.

due to an inadequate understanding of our individual worth to God or because of a deficient appreciation of the depth of God's love for us. I believe our biggest misstep would be in the phrase "all that trouble"—a choice of words that shows a fundamental misunderstanding of God's nature.

Yes, God is eternal and ultimate joy, with unspeakable depths of happiness, but the nature of that happiness is not in pleasure, which is what I naturally picture, but in *sacrifice*. I wish it were not true, but in my own heart the word *sacrifice* typically suggests misery and drudgery—not joy. When I have to fix some sort of mess that my children have created, I am not generally singing in ecstasy but trying to maintain a pleasant demeanor to cover up my lack of pleasure at having to do a bothersome chore that has interrupted what I otherwise was doing at the moment. In the end I do not mind having to perform these fixes because I love my children, and helping with their troubles is part of that wonderful privilege of raising them. However, this positive attitude is neither my first nor my natural inclination but is rather the attitude I work hard to attain despite my personal dislike of sacrificial suffering.

God is different—because His very nature is different. As scripture and theologians throughout church history have told us, God does not *have* love. He *is* love. And His love is fundamentally sacrificial, meaning that *He* is fundamentally sacrificial. It would be inaccurate to state that He is willing to sacrifice for us because He loves us, as that phrase would suggest a distinction between love and sacrifice, as if sacrifice were a product of His love. It is only accurate to say that His love *is* sacrificial—they are one and the same thing—in the same way that water is wet. Therefore, because He does love us so much, individually with as much intensity as corporately (as in the story of Trey above), the idea that He would *not* go to any length to save any single one of us would be to misunderstand the fundamental essence of His character. We therefore should not be surprised by the words of C. S. Lewis.

In the end, we can have no true pleasure or fulfillment without developing a heart of generosity, in which the needs of others come before our own. When we picture heaven, I think that we most naturally think of it as a place of indescribable happiness, of a permanent, overwhelmingly fulfilling joy, absent of pain and suffering: everyone will be "enjoying" the pleasure of eternal bliss. I believe all of that is true, but the *nature* of that bliss will be one of sacrifice, not self-centeredness. None of us will get to heaven and find that everyone there will be trying to make us happy; rather, we will get there and find ourselves trying to help make *them* happy—that will be what brings us joy.

In light of all of the above, the phrase "all that trouble" really has no meaning. In my own mind there seems to be no way to describe the passion, the cross, or any of the innumerable other costs that Jesus experienced as anything but *a lot of trouble* on my behalf. But my attitude simply shows how far I have yet to mature in my faith, as it implies that those godly deeds are an exception—a *contrast,* if you will—to what God typically is experiencing and doing in heaven. God's deeds performed for our salvation and happiness are not exceptions at all; they are exactly in keeping with His constant nature, His moment-by-moment activities, His current and unending day-to-day life so to speak; in other words, they are typical examples of His Being. For Him, there is no trouble in all that trouble. As George MacDonald so aptly puts it, "When he died on the cross, he did that, in the wild weather of his outlying provinces in the torture of the body of his revelation, which he had done at home in glory and gladness."[13]

As I get older, heaven gets nearer, and I spend more of my prayer time meditating on, bathing in, and marveling at God's sacrificial nature, reflecting on how I want to adopt that nature as my own. At some point in my future I *must* adopt that character if I am going to fit into heaven, so delaying the transformation does not make much sense to me anymore. The absence of "all that trouble" in God's character seems such an amazing concept to me, because I am still learning to possess and live a life in which there is no such thing as reluctance to lay down my life for others. My ultimate goal is that going to "trouble" for someone who is in need will no longer be any trouble at all, no matter how costly, but will simply be the natural and joyful outpouring of the person I have become.

Now *that* is something worth meditating on ... and worth praying for.

---

[13] George MacDonald, *Unspoken Sermons,* "The Creation of Christ."

21

Rhinoceros

He took it for a walk.

Andrew and Brie were happily married, mutually devoted, and raising a family with everything seemingly heading in the right direction. Andrew, talented in what he did for a living, worked hard for many years and, as is appropriate, received more and more compliments for his achievements on the job. Unfortunately, those accolades went to his ego, and gradually— almost immeasurably slowly at first—he found himself developing a sense of self-importance, such that the easy and obvious rewards of work became more important to him than the more difficult and sometimes less-obvious rewards of marriage and of raising teenage children. He began to neglect his family, spending ever more time at the office, increasingly relegating to Brie all the work of running the household and raising the now older children. She spent most of her time alone ... or alone with the kids. When he initially approached the marriage, he could not have wanted things to go this way, but over time his priorities got the better of him, and his marriage crumbled—all for rewards that, in the final analysis, held very little meaning.

This scenario is commonplace and occurs to men and women alike. The details might differ from person to person, but the story line is fundamentally the same. Regretfully, I have seen it in the lives of my patients on too many occasions.

It is easy to define our lives and develop a sense of inner meaning in terms of our interests, our goals, our commitments, our passions, and the like. Our culture certainly promotes such an approach, but in my view, this outlook completely misses the mark.

Each of us has a core, an innermost heart—what you could call our private sanctuary, and whatever resides in there is what defines us. This core can be a very misunderstood realm. Because it lies at the very center of our being, it typically is thought of as small and well encapsulated, something we can protect and control. I believe such a perspective is mistaken. That inner heart is enormous. Ask any parent who is overflowing with pride for a child, or a lover who is bursting with love for his or her espoused—the total capacity of our inner heart is remarkable.

That core is where God means to reside, both because that is where He naturally belongs and because that is the only place where He fits, as He is too big for any of the other, more superficial layers of our heart. He belongs only in our deepest realm.

God also is not satisfied with token visitation. Rather, He wants to enter in *fully*, so He created our core unimaginably vast. ... and voraciously hungry—it hungers, after all, for Him. Almost with a will of its own, it is a cavernous expanse whose appetite is huge, and we therefore cannot hope to have the strength to control it on our own. For better or for worse, our core relentlessly craves whatever we most desire—or, perhaps better put, whatever we worship. If we most desire our Lord, then our heart will pursue Him with great fervor. In contrast, if we desire other things more than God, be it wealth, power, beauty, fame, comfort, pleasure, reputation, or another person, then our inner heart will pursue those things with the same fervor ... and leave God behind, no matter our efforts to the contrary. In this latter case, like a toddler trying to take a leashed rhinoceros for a stroll, slowly but surely our core will drag us haplessly along to places we initially might not want to go, perhaps leading us to say or do or believe things we never would have thought imaginable. Or that rhinoceros might simply lie down and refuse to budge for awhile, leaving us spiritually stagnant for a period of time, wasting our years on priorities that ultimately get us nowhere.

No, our inner heart is not some small, private, quaint sanctuary; rather, it is a vast, untamed realm that God never expected us to fully conquer. Influence? Yes. Feed? Yes. Discipline? Yes. Guide, direct, and rule for awhile? Yes, again. But *conquer*? No, not possible. It is more powerful than we are. It was designed to be God's home, and nothing colossal enough in size and strength to house the infinite can be expected to be completely subdued and kept under control by someone like you or me. Our hope, then, is not to try to subdue it on our own power but to aim it in the right direction—and toward God is the right direction. Only God has the power to tame it.

But to tame our inner core, God must fill it.

And He enters into that realm primarily through prayer—and best of all through prayer that longs for His *presence*. God wants us not merely to follow and obey Him but to *love* Him, which is the essential and final purpose of life. After all, while on earth we are in a courtship with Him, not in boot camp. He is our espoused, not our boss or drill sergeant. And He wants to *live* in our heart, being intimately and tangibly present, not just set up shop there or have us simply think about Him there.

The dilemma—and what gives us great pause—is that God has a mind of His own: He has plans, ideas, hopes, and goals for us. He is not subject to our every whim or fancy, and we cannot command Him to go in any direction we prefer to go. This presents us with a major problem: Do we dare invite this dynamic, unpredictable, and very willful Being into the center of our lives? Who knows what He might do! Would it not be safer to fill our core with *things* such as the material goals I listed above, rather than with a *Being*? We cannot control God, but we can control things ... or at least in our pride we think we can.

Ironically, therein lies the ultimate trap, the fatal flaw in such logic. We tend to have the mistaken notion that because we are the ones choosing an inanimate goal such as money or success or whatever, we therefore can exert control over that goal. It is, after all, *our* goal, and it has no mind of its own! But alas, it is not the goal that betrays us—it is our inner heart that does so. We should not delude ourselves here. As I mention above, our inner heart is stronger than our mental will, so if we aim our heart in a direction other than toward God, it will drag us to places we will regret, like that toddler with the rhinoceros. We might achieve our earthly goals, but where will we end up in the process? This errant journey might be imperceptibly slow at first, but we eventually will end up somewhere we did not initially intend to be. If you doubt me, look at the lives of many of the rich and famous. Or simply be patient, live out your years pursuing things, and then look at your own life.

Andrew pursued his earthly rewards, enjoying his importance in the eyes of others and of himself. Neglecting the priority of marriage and family, he started walking that rhinoceros. Although I know that Andrew had not wanted his life to turn out this way, he had put the wrong priority in his inner heart, and the goodness in his life dissolved around him. Attempting to be master of his destiny, he ironically lost control of his life. The rhinoceros had dragged him to where he had not wanted to go.

Like Andrew, we do not have to completely abandon God in order to end up with such a fate. Rather, we can simply put God in second place, still trying to love and follow Him while in reality wanting something else more—a priority that never turns out well.

We can take great comfort in knowing that God has the power to fully tame our inner heart and that He will *always* lead us to places that are best for our happiness and for our good. Simply put, our prayers *must* take us to a place of complete trust. Personally, I know that I frequently do not succeed in that endeavor from one day to the next, but I try hard to do so.

I do not want to take a rhinoceros for a walk.

22

God Truly Does Answer Our Prayers

Grace stared at her mom with panic in her eyes. "No! No! Don't let him!" she cried out with a voice that broke my heart. I, of course, was "him," the horrible villain who was about to perform a painful procedure on Grace—a procedure necessary but far beyond her understanding. Grace had an abscess that needed to be drained or she could become seriously ill. She wanted to have the painful abscess fixed—that was clear—but not in the way I was going to fix it. All she could see was unfairness and pain, and her conviction was certain: the procedure was unnecessary. There *must* be a better way. As adults, Grace's mother and I both saw why it was unavoidable. The abscess was big enough to demand drainage, yet not big enough to justify the risks of general anesthesia, so a shot of local anesthetic follow by incision with a scalpel was the best way. I was confident and at peace with the decision—but I felt awful about having to do this to Grace, who could appreciate neither the gravity of her current situation nor the future harm that would come if her abscess was ignored. There simply was no other way to proceed.

Her mother, full of mixed emotions, cried and tried her best to comfort and reassure her daughter. Grace's "prayer" to her mom at that moment was to fix the problem but keep me from doing what I was about to do. Her mom, wiser and more far-sighted than her daughter, would answer Grace's prayer in a better way, but in a way that Grace could not yet understand. And in the midst of the drama, the glory of what I witnessed between the two was that *Grace did not reject her mother* because of the difference in opinion. Indeed, Grace still trusted and clung to her mother. After the procedure was finished, while still in tears, she hugged her mom even harder, still trusting in her mom's protection and providence. In the end, Grace's prayer to her mom was answered exactly as it should have been, with her mother protecting her as Grace had requested, thereby preventing a disaster much worse than the pain of the procedure. But Grace was still many years away from understanding that fact.

So it should be with us. Prayer is not a token activity. No genuine prayer you have ever uttered has fallen on deaf ears. God *always* responds to our requests, although His answer is often not to our understanding or liking. When we pray, He acts. Our lives, and even human history, are thereby changed. How this works is beyond me, but God states that this is true, and I am not inclined to doubt Him. Consider the mystery: God is not changeable, and He knows what we will pray before we utter a word. He does not need our information, our authority, our insight, our vote, or anything else from us in order to answer any prayer we utter. Yet *He does not jest* when He states that our prayers count— they are not meaningless rituals of devotion that our Father ignores while He pats us on the head for good effort and does what He wants anyway. Nor are our prayers irrelevant because God already knows the future outcome. Prayers change lives, influence events, usher in God's interventions, and alter history. Do not try to figure this one out theologically but take it as gospel truth, and let it spur you to spend more time on your knees.

At this point many Christians legitimately ask why it *seems* that God often ignores our prayers. The response to this question, like most things in the Christian life, is not straightforward and should never be portrayed as such. Some prayers are answered yes. Others "Yes, but not in the way you expect." Still others are simply answered no, or perhaps "Yes, but not yet," as was the case in my own family. Some answers to prayer might not be known until we reach heaven, as the answer is given after we have died. But *none* are ignored. In each of the possible answers God can give, the crucial issue is not whether we can figure out the reasoning behind or the consequences of His answers— Grace certainly was not yet wise enough to understand my answer to her medical need—but whether we have a strong enough relationship that we can *trust* Him.

Consider Anna, the prophetess mentioned in Luke 2:36–38 who greeted the newborn Jesus in the temple. After a seven-year marriage that likely started in her teens, she was a widow until the age of eighty-four years old, which means that she likely was a widow for over sixty years. Imagine that for a moment. Sixty years of patience, of waiting. Why did God have her wait so long? Why not let her be a widow for one year and then have Jesus appear at the temple? Looking back, you and I might be able to think of several reasons, but Anna did not have the luxury of looking back. She was simply living one day at a time, praying faithfully but not necessarily with any specific answer to her "Why?" questions. She could not know how long she would live, and she likely wondered why she lived so long in an age when so many died young. Unlike Simeon, there is no mention in scripture that Anna had been told by God that she would stay alive until the Messiah arrived. Her "purpose" in life therefore might have been unclear. Yet she loved and trusted—for sixty years or more—that there was some purpose to her struggle.

In my own family, we only had to wait approximately ten years to find out the answer to our prayers, but even that felt like ten lifetimes. My oldest daughter, Rachel, has a form of autism, and my wife, Jeanie, and I therefore had to make some difficult career choices and sacrifices at several points during Rachel's younger years in the late 1980s and early 1990s. At that time high-functioning autism was not a widely recognized medical condition, so none of the numerous medical specialists we consulted could give us an answer to Rachel's pervasive and confusing problems. It was extremely difficult for us as parents to cope, as we were blind, suffering, and seemed to have such little hope. We tried to make headway with her upbringing but to little avail, and even when her diagnosis was finally realized after she turned ten years old, we could not make headway, as there were no proven treatment guidelines for such a newly recognized medical condition. We attempted to arrange and implement some of the rare remediation programs that existed at the time, but we kept hitting one brick wall after another. For years, even after we had the correct diagnosis, nothing seemed to make sense, everything appeared to be going wrong, and each attempt to help Rachel turned out to be a dead end. We were constantly discouraged, and I cannot count the number of Sunday church services we spent in tears. Although we tried to tell ourselves otherwise, it felt to us that our prayers were being ignored, even refuted. My personality is such that I do not tend to rant and rave at God, but those years were a great struggle for me.

It wasn't until more than ten years after Jeanie and I made those career sacrifices mentioned above, when all of our struggles came to a head, that God's carefully laid plans became evident: out of necessity, my wife Jeanie, who also is a physician, started developing a treatment program for Rachel, and Rachel thereby received better help than we could have expected. In retrospect, the prior options we had been seeking would not have helped her, although we could not have seen that at the time. The brick walls were God's way of steering us in the right direction. In addition, Jeanie wrote her program during the earliest years in the development of treatment programs for children with high-functioning autism. She was able to consolidate her programs into a book that has been internationally received, and she found a career path that allowed her to help patients with autism while still being able to stay home most of the time with our four daughters. None of this would have happened if our earlier prayers had been answered in the way we had wanted. Even looking back now, I do not see any willful blindness on our part that kept us from seeing God's carefully laid plans. He knew what was needed to answer our prayers, and He made it happen. He did not accomplish His will in an easy fashion—it was difficult beyond words—but an easy solution would have taken away our opportunity to grow. We simply had to wait, to work, and to exercise our trust while waiting for God's timing.

One could question why He let us hit brick walls instead of simply providing us with the answers. I am not so wise that I can fully answer that question, but here is what I believe. First, as trusting as I like to think I am, I harbor no illusions about how hard God has to work to get me to rely on Him rather than on myself. It can take years of struggle to break through my stubborn habit of self-sufficiency. Second, each of those brick walls specifically turned out to be necessary for Jeanie to develop her program. Each dead end was a dead end *for a reason*. Brick wall by brick wall Jeanie learned about programs for high-functioning autism, why some approaches work and others do not. The exposure to ineffective and counterproductive programs, as well as to good programs, made Jeanie vastly more insightful into the whole field of autism. She has lectured on the subject internationally, and without those "brick wall" experiences she would never have been so helpful when addressing her audiences.

Of course, many prayers are lifted up for issues far greater, more complex, and more devastating than the ones I mention above. My wife and I were fortunate in the end to be able to see God's plans regarding Rachel—we have not been so fortunate with other calamities our family has suffered. Worse yet are atrocities involving entire nations or peoples, about which Christians all over the globe pray—and yet it can seem like things never change.

But don't they? Our sense of time is short, but God works over generations. The history of nations moves and evolves slowly, but it does change. In addition, the effects of God's interventions in the lives of each individual within those countries happen every day, just like they do in our own lives. When we pray, we pray not just for the countries as a whole but even more so for the people within those countries. God is always working in their individual lives, during each and every minute, in ways you and I will never see. Do we trust that His providence is merciful to those people? Even if their national crisis seems so dismal? Do we think that God has abandoned them just because *we* cannot see His works?

In scripture we are described as young children in the presence of a Father. In my clinic I have witnessed the interaction of countless children with their parents, and I have *never* seen a young child who understands or agrees with many of the medical decisions the parents make: having to be examined by a strange and frightening doctor when the child is sick, getting blood tests or shots, undergoing lifesaving but painful procedures, taking bad-testing medicines, being told to abstain from destructive behaviors, having privileges revoked, having sports participation stopped due to medical problems, etc. The child often feels betrayed or abandoned by the parents, even when the parents are 100 percent loving and correct. In terms of our relationship with our Father, we are like those children. You and I cannot even see one hour into our futures. Why then are we surprised that God's answers are often difficult to understand or take longer than we like? The young children in my clinic typically do not have the developmental maturity to submit to their parents' wisdom ... you and I, on the other hand, *do* have the capacity to do that with God.

Grace is older and has healed from her abscess procedure. There will always be a scar and possibly some discomfort at the incision site, but she now lives a vibrant, happy life. In the case of our own confusing episodes of suffering, God desires the same recovery for us all. The important thing—and the hardest truth for us to see during a time of crisis—is that God always aims to bring us to a point of love and fulfillment. Let us pray that we always remain open to such an outcome.

23

Transition

I wonder how many sets of eyes have looked up at their parents over the years during doctor visits with absolute shock and lack of comprehension. I am speaking, of course, about the eyes of little children who do not understand their parents' words or actions. Every parent throughout history has seen that same look.

It is no surprise to anyone that the transition from infancy to adulthood is a difficult process. The infant and the young toddler believe, with complete innocence and sincerity of heart—and through no fault of their own—that they are the center of the world. How could they not think so? They ask and then receive. They need and are supplied. They disrupt, and the world around them changes and accommodates. They hurt, and they are the first to garner attention. Who could possibly criticize them for their egocentric worldview that says, "It's all about me!"

I often have reflected in my clinic, especially when I see a parent properly correct a child's behavior, about how unfair and difficult life must appear to those children at that instant. These children look at the parent with genuine confusion and hurt. With no understanding of why such unintelligible, unwelcome, sometimes painful, and seemingly arbitrary rules, disciplines, or medical treatments are being imposed "from above", the child must feel confused, emotionally hurt, and personally betrayed by a parent who is supposed to love them and be loved in return. Worse yet, the parents typically can offer only a short and—to the child—woefully inadequate reason for the painful event. Pause for a moment and put yourself in the child's shoes, and you get the idea. No wonder they get angry and cry so loudly. I, for one, do not blame them.

Yet the transition to maturity *must* be made. We all know grown-ups who never completed that process of personal growth, and it is not a pretty sight. At some point, between the toddler stage and adulthood, the child is expected to change from egocentric to othercentric, from selfish to selfless, from "you sacrifice for me" to "I sacrifice for you." And that transition is undeniably painful, full of hard lessons, bathed in childhood confusion, and generally unwelcome. Young children "don't know what they don't know," and therefore most of life's important lessons are unexpected and incomprehensible, making their lives feel overwhelmingly complex with unnecessary suffering. They do not recognize their personal shortcomings—and would not understand them even if recognized—and consequently do not see the need for correction and guidance.

It is easy to see how all of the above resembles our spiritual journey. When you and I first choose to follow Jesus, we cannot possibly see all the ways in which we must spiritually mature, and like the children described above, we would not understand those ways even if we did see them. So when God's trials come our way, they initially will seem to us unexpected and inexplicable, likely even irrelevant to how we understand our lives at the time. But God is wise and knows what we need. In no way is He a cruel Father who heartlessly makes unreasonable and arbitrary demands of us. But He likewise is not a neglectful Father who equally heartlessly ignores our immaturities, thereby permitting us to remain spiritual toddlers all our lives—a fate that would be similarly cruel. He wants us to grow such that we will have even greater joy, and He is willing and able to lead us through trials—even painful trials—to help us do just that. Those trials will be hard to understand at first, and we should not be surprised that we do not like them or welcome them, but we should want them to occur. Such trials go against our fallen natures, but that is good: God makes it abundantly clear in scripture that He wants us to grow up to be like Him.

In terms of my faith, I am not yet fully mature, but I am mature enough to *know* that I am not yet fully mature. So I understand and accept the unavoidable fact that God has more lessons to bring my way, and I recognize ahead of time that I will not like them when they come. Is that because God is mean? Or that I have a pessimistic attitude toward faith? On the contrary! I tend to be an undying optimist, but I do not want to remain a spiritual toddler. I know that my upcoming trials are for my good and for my joy. I prefer to have my Father help me to grow in the ways that He knows best rather than for me to remain immature throughout my spiritual adulthood.

Like the children in my clinic, I am in transition ... from spiritual infancy to spiritual maturity. When things get tough, I do not want to gaze up at my Father with a look of shock and betrayal, to turn away from Him, or to stop praying. I might cry, perhaps even scream at Him, but I want to continue trusting in and talking with Him. The parents in my clinic know that the lessons through which they take their children are for the children's benefit, and the parents desperately want their children to continue trusting and talking with them.

Would God want anything less from us?

24

Patients and Patience

What does a primary care physician spend more time doing than everything else combined?

We *wait.*

Yes we, like our patients, wait for test results to return, wait for treatments to take effect, and so forth. That kind of waiting is not what I am writing about. Greater and more important by far is the time we spend waiting for our numerous reluctant patients to adopt lifesaving lifestyle changes, to take their illnesses more seriously, to become motivated, to stay with their treatment programs, to admit to us when they do not follow instructions (something we usually figure out anyway), to open up about personal aspects of their health that might hold the key to their recovery, or simply to return to our clinic for follow up. Physicians can teach, encourage, exhort, and attempt to motivate those reluctant patients in any number of ways, but we cannot choose for them. We cannot make them care.

For physicians who have a heart for their patients—and the vast percentage of us do—this waiting can be hard to endure. Having studied and witnessed firsthand the long-term consequences of neglected disease gives physicians a fairly accurate idea of the suffering that awaits these reluctant patients, and that foresight weighs heavily on us. I often have felt something akin to desperation when trying to help patients see their upcoming fate if they do not take their health seriously or if they only take token steps to correct what requires big strides of commitment.

There are numerous reasons why patients minimize the significance of their illnesses: reluctance to change, denial, fear, preference of the pleasures of their current lifestyle over the discipline of a healthier one, health simply is not a priority, and so forth. Some reasons are understandable and legitimate, while others are harder to comprehend, but in none of these situations is it my place to judge or criticize. I simply encourage, teach, emphasize that I am always ready to jump on board if and when the patient decides to change ... and I wait.

I also empathize.

After all, in terms of my spiritual health, I am like my patients with their physical health. Throughout scripture God spends far more time patiently waiting than He does anything else, and things are no different in our world today. God sees with great clarity the short term and long term consequences if we neglect our spiritual health, and that foresight weighs heavily on Him. So He waits for us to take our spiritual lives as seriously as I ask my patients to take their physical lives. Unfortunately, I suspect most of us are reluctant spiritual patients to some degree or other. Physicians such as myself—as well as parents, caretakers, or anyone else who cares for others and tries to get them to take their health seriously—have the least excuse for delaying and neglecting our spiritual lives, but we often do so anyway.

In my medical practice, usually the first step my reluctant patients must take in order to take charge of their health is to see me in clinic and open up about their reluctance so that we can figure out how to proceed. I enjoy those clinic visits beyond compare—they can literally make my day. Regarding our spiritual lives, I believe God is the same. The first step you and I must take—if we desire to take our spiritual lives more seriously and thereby live godlier lives—is to open up to Him in prayer, ask for a change in heart, and most of all, seek His presence. I believe such prayers are His favorite kind.

They certainly make His day.

25

Hunger? Thirst?

It was not going well for young Zach.

His mother continued to use methamphetamines—as she had during her entire pregnancy with him—and she generally neglected his care. He was barely clothed, hardly washed, and poorly fed. In sum, it was not a happy home. Fortunately, Zach's plight was made known to the local authorities, so he was removed from the house at one year of age and was placed in foster care with a wonderful family that I knew in my clinic. I therefore had the privilege of taking on Zach as a new patient. A few years later Zach was adopted by his new family, and I therefore also have had the privilege of watching him grow up for the past eighteen years.

Before he was taken into foster care, Zach was on a dismal trajectory. Without the benefit of appropriate parental love and care, he clearly had become depressed. At his first clinic visit, soon after being placed with his new family, I found him to be withdrawn, passive, and lacking in facial expression. Through no fault of his own, his mother had been taking him down a very dark path with a strong likelihood of lifelong depression, horrible self-esteem, and high risk of future drug abuse.[14]

Within a few short months of living with his foster family, Zach was a different person: happy, giggling, animated, interactive, and very attached to his new mother. Of course, many trials were yet to come—children like Zach have at least as many struggles as any other children—but he now was given all of the emotional, psychological, and physical tools necessary to successfully navigate those difficult times. Zach currently is just short of twenty years old, and he has become a wonderful young man.

I have taken care of many such foster children, rescued from homes of abuse and neglect where life was cruel and inhospitable, and absorbed into homes where love is the norm. In their new environment, wherein they are encouraged, nourished both emotionally and spiritually, provided with sustenance, hugged (literally and figuratively), and saturated with parental care and patience, these children change. This road of redemption is—for the new parents as well as for the child—always a long and arduous one, but it is worthwhile, often beginning with despair and ending with joy. Although not all such children turn out well, most grow up to be totally different people than they were otherwise destined to be. Never have I found something more rewarding in my medical practice than the privilege of witnessing this transition.

God says that we should "hunger" and "thirst" for His righteousness. He did not say that we should merely "strive

---

[14] It is important to emphasize that a tremendous number of children who are born into such homes grow up to be wonderful, productive, happy adults. But the majority of such children do not fare so well.

for" or "hope for" or "aim for" righteousness, although those goals also are important. Hunger and thirst are not passions or virtues, or even desires. They are not primarily, or even secondarily, intellectual, and they well up in us independent of our will, in that we do not choose at any given moment to be hungry or thirsty. These two characteristics are *instincts*—gut-level, primal, involuntary drives that move us to act out of a need for survival. We *strive* for things that are personally important to us. We *hunger* and *thirst* for things because our nature demands it of us.

Jesus says that the latter should be true of our relationship with God. He is not content that we merely choose Him. He desires that our longing for Him should instinctively well up in us like the passion for survival. I cannot speak for you, but my problem is not that I do not already know this truth. I simply have trouble living it out.

None of the above constitutes groundbreaking theological insight, but it is difficult to make a reality in our lives. The question for us is not how to get such hungering and thirsting into our heads and hearts but how to get them into our guts. Instincts are intensely powerful drives, and to develop new ones requires a wholesale change in character—actually a wholesale change in *being*—not just a change in mind-set or priorities. Such a feat is not accomplished in a day. Neither is it accomplished by ourselves. And, although this transformation ultimately brings joy beyond description (on earth as well as in heaven), the process also will dig up obstacles, many of which *we* have created, that resist such change. These obstacles have to die. I believe this is one of the ways in which Jesus means we have to "die to ourselves."

Ultimately God wants to change us into new creatures with new instincts, not just people who think and feel and choose differently. For that transformation to succeed, we must willingly let God take us through the tests and experiences that reveal our weaknesses and disordered passions—a process that is unwelcome to any rational human being. Speaking for myself, I readily admit that I would prefer to avoid such trials and to fall in love with God simply by being happy and sensing His presence, a preference that vastly underestimates the amount of work He has to do in me. God wants to *heal* me and make me new, not simply make me feel happy.

It is living these truths, not knowing them, that ultimately counts. Knowing them requires a simple thirty-minute Bible study. Living them requires a lifetime of devotion. It is impossible for us to instill a hunger and a thirst for righteousness on our own, because we cannot create drives at such a deep level simply by choice—instincts cannot be self-created—and because our fallen natures work against us. In the end, it is God who must create this change in us, and primarily through prayer does that happen, because only by His enduring *presence* in our lives can our instincts slowly change. We can *act* godly through choice. We can *become* godly only by saturation. It is by soaking in His presence—during prayer and in our day-to-day lives as God increasingly becomes our constant companion—that His heart becomes ours. As I said above, that takes time. For Zach and other such fortunate foster children it is not so much the lessons and corrections from their new parents that make the difference in their lives, but rather the environment of familial acceptance and love that drenches and slowly permeates the children's personalities, such that their fundamental characters change.

In the end, we change through saturation, through the constancy of His presence, more than from any other aspect of the Christian life. Nothing less suffices. Think of petrified wood, wherein a tree changes entirely into stone. Such a complete transformation cannot happen unless the fallen tree "bathes" in the ground for a substantial amount of time. As the tree soaks in the soil through the years, the minerals from the soil slowly replace the wood until the wood literally turns into stone—bit by bit over millennia the tree becomes wholly different than what it was. God wants to do the same with us. He desires to have us soak in His presence until we are new creatures with new instincts, having absorbed His very nature.

Once tasted, God's presence becomes like a sumptuous meal: something we hunger for. But our degree of hunger will be directly proportional to the amount of God's presence to which we have grown accustomed; if we only have experience a little of Him and do not continue to seek out His company, then our hunger for Him lasts only a short while, and our love for Him will fade. New instincts will not have had time to develop. But a lifetime of seeking out and enjoying His presence during our times of prayer—and during the rest of our day as the distinction between prayer life and regular life disappears—will change our nature and instill into our guts a voracious hunger and thirst that will make our hearts full and will bring us peace.

Such a life is something to be lived—and something worth living for.

26

Steps

It was so busy in the emergency room at the moment that patients were lying on beds lining the hallway—never an optimal choice but sometimes unavoidable in a busy hospital during an epidemic. I was working an extra shift in the ER as an admitting physician and had just finished evaluating and writing admission orders for two complicated patients. I then found myself walking down the corridor past the patients lining the hall, daydreaming and thinking to myself that at any moment, with my next step, my pager could go off again or someone in the hallway could medically decompensate right in front of me. As a physician, life with a pager among seriously ill patients is always unpredictable, and our professional duties often are not under our control. We must be ready, at any moment, to turn our full attention to an unexpected demand placed upon us.

In like manner, in our faith we all carry a spiritual pager, we all walk among the spiritually ill (I consider myself one of them!), and God can page us at any time for one sacrificial task or another. But fortunately God knows our own needs just as much as the needs of the person we are meant to help, and He never pages us without having our interests also at heart, no matter how dire the circumstances seem to us. Even though His page usually is in service of one of His children, it is always for our good as well, even if we cannot see it at the time.

While daydreaming during the moment I described above walking down the hallway, my imagination wandered, and I pictured Jesus walking on earth two thousand years ago, along the dusty streets in sandals, surrounded by people in desperate spiritual need. In a sense, He had His own "pager." He was ready at each step for His Father to bring something new and unexpected His way, and He did not fear what might come. He was always open to a sudden change in His daily agenda. As I was walking between those patients in the hallway, that picture of Jesus gave me a renewed appreciation for the necessity to have God's heart always as my own and to be in constant prayer at every moment so that I will not be taken by surprise when my Father brings physical or spiritual demands into my life. Each step I take then becomes a miniature devotion, a prayer so to speak—and everyone who crosses my path, whether pleasant or not, becomes an instrument of God to mold and shape me into His likeness.

Prayer—at least genuine prayer—changes us for the better and brings God's heart deeper into our own. We should desire an abundance of such prayer. So just imagine: every physical step we take in our lives as a prayer. A million tiny devotionals ... every day. Each stride becoming a purposeful openness to His call. Whether consciously concentrating on God at the moment or simply focusing on the needs around us with a generous heart and with God as our companion, such a prayerful life of service is a blessing that our world desperately needs ...

... and a blessing that we equally need.

27

Sacred

There is a sense of the sacred in a medical clinic room. This sense is subtle and often overlooked, but it is there nonetheless. What is discussed between patient and doctor in the clinic is treated with the same privacy and respect as anything said in a confessional.[15] Nothing gets out. There should be total trust within that clinic room. The things I hear from my patients about their private lives, struggles, hopes, and experiences are astoundingly personal and vulnerable, and I am honored by the degree to which my patients place their trust in me. A physician with compassion will routinely experience profound depths of honesty and openness from patients, as is appropriate for the context but is nevertheless quite humbling—something one could even call sacred.

When the relationship and trust between patient and physician is strong, there is no need for the patient to hold back regarding any issue that relates to his or her health. Although there are exceptions, it is surprisingly easy for a physician to sense when a patient is lying, shading the truth, or holding back. Typically

---

[15] Irrespective of whether one believes in the practice of confessionals, it is well recognized that personal confessions therein are kept fully private.

there is something transparent in the demeanor of a patient who is trying to be nontransparent. It never serves the patient well.

We should keep the same in mind when we pray. God should hear from us the same honesty and confession that I hear from my patients, no matter our humiliation or reluctance. We should never try to pray with deception. In doing so we only harm ourselves, and God can see through our facades anyway. As a physician I have seen how the most painful and embarrassing topic a patient discusses with me often turns out to be the key to his or her healing and happiness. So it is with prayer. We should never hold back in God's presence but should tell Him all. Our time with Him is sacred. He is absolutely trustworthy to guard our hearts, and we desperately need His healing touch ...

... a healing for which He has already paid.

28

Tears

Maria was crying ... softly and without losing control, but she was too heartbroken to stop. We were discussing her young son who once more had fallen prey to drugs and was now in jail ... again. He, in truth, was a nice kid, always delightful when in my clinic, and I enjoyed his genuine personality and sensitive spirit—a truly great character. If only he could manage to avoid drugs, he could have a wonderful and happy life ahead and spend more time with his mother. Easy to say, but not so easy to accomplish—addictions have tremendous power.

In Maria's eyes I saw a haunted pain—and an unfathomable depth of care for her son. The fact that she would do *anything* to get her son out of his cycle of trouble was written all over her face. No sacrifice would have been too great. But her desire to help him did have that one unavoidable limitation: it could not extend past the leading edge of her son's mind. He had free choice. Maria could not choose *for* him, no matter the depth of her passion, as his choice for health had to come from his own heart, and he was not to that point yet. So Maria prayed, waited, helped when her son would allow, never lost hope for him, guided where she could ... and she cried.

Over the years as my faith has grown, I have noticed an irony that I did not expect to find. In my early years as a Christian, I used to think that my heart would become more at peace and more content as my prayer life deepened. To an extent that is true. Yet in many ways the opposite has happened: I cry more, not less. When observing human behavior, I experience deeper pain, not shallower. The closer I get to God's heart, the more I taste His desire to draw us all to Himself ... and our stubborn habit of spurning that gift.

With all due reverence to God and with recognition of the obvious differences between God and humankind, I believe that the Lord is much like Maria. I sense His "no-holding-back" dedication to sacrifice everything in order to bring us into the joy of His presence, but I also see more clearly how I, and the rest of His children, can fall prey to our own brand of worldly addictions— things that separate us from Him. This breaks God's heart. You and I can become addicted to the false promises of this world, promises that claim to provide happiness but instead simply anesthetize our spirit and dull us down, separating us from the only source of true fulfillment. We imprison ourselves—some of us to a greater extent, some to a lesser, but none of us is immune.

Fortunately at such times God remains potent and active, working for our deliverance from our self-imposed prisons, but He will never overwhelm our free will. Instead, He helps us, hopes for us, guides us, waits for us ... and He hurts for us. Because we do not see God's face directly, it can be hard to imagine what He must look like at those times. I believe the Lord would look something akin to Maria—a fruitful image upon which to meditate during prayer ...

... and a great source of motivation for us to repent.

29

Complicated

Another typical day on the cardiac wing of our local hospital: busy, hectic, and medically difficult. I was sitting at the computer workstation finishing up a daily progress note on one of my critically ill patients when I overheard Stella, an experienced and at the moment very busy nurse who was taking care of yet another difficult problem, comment to a colleague with a bit of a chuckle, "Remember when life used to be so much easier?" There was no complaint or resentment in her voice but simply an accurate understanding of how hospital inpatient medical care, and medicine in general, has changed.

On average, and to no one's surprise, hospitalized patients today are significantly more ill and complex than even just a few decades ago, and fewer patients are being admitted for simple, straightforward reasons. This ever-increasing complexity is an inevitable consequence of improved medical care: Patients are surviving acute crises that used to be lethal, and many formerly terminal diseases are now managed as chronic illnesses. Patients with critical conditions therefore are living longer and are developing even more medical problems that further complicate their already complex health. Fortunately, some of these illnesses overlap in terms of symptoms and treatments, allowing physicians to address more than one condition with a single treatment. But a large number of diseases are at odds with each other, meaning that the treatment of one illness can make another illness worse, and vice versa. For many of the most chronically ill patients, physicians now have to perform a medical tightrope act, striking a balance between equally lifesaving treatments that nevertheless directly oppose one another—a quandary I personally have faced many times. Such tightrope walking is very difficult, and it can be emotionally, intellectually, and even physically taxing.

As we grow older, our entire lives can follow this same trend. Not that the lives of young people are always simple and straightforward, but almost invariably life becomes more complicated as we age. There are more concerns to worry about, more conflicts and crises competing for our attention, more loose ends that need to be tied up, and frequently it can feel overwhelming. As in medical care, our attempts to fix one thorny situation in our lives can make another situation worse, or vice versa. Such complexity is, in my view, to some extent inevitable—an inescapable result of leading an active life. That is, of course, unless we choose to become isolated, uncaring islands unto ourselves ... a choice we should avoid like the plague.

Stella, despite her tongue-in-cheek, humorously intended comment, in reality would never want to go back to the old days in medicine, comfortably simpler though they might be, as that would represent a loss of all the wonderful medical progress for the last thirty years. In this I agree with her. She is thankful for her complicated responsibilities. Similarly in my own case, despite my occasional lamentation about how harried my personal life has become, I would never want to go back to my own easier days, as that would erase all of the wonderful choices and commitments I have made over the years.

But that leaves us with the question of how we view our hectic lives. As a good thing? Or a bad thing? Perhaps both? I certainly do not believe that a harried life with many worries is something to be sought after. But is it something we should regret? Something to bemoan?

Not entirely.

There definitely is a tipping point in everyone's life when things become sufficiently complex and stressful that simplification of one's life becomes essential. I have advised many of my patients to undergo that simplification, and at times, I have done the same. However, even when that simplification is accomplished, my experience from observing the lives of my patients (not to mention my own life) is that life still remains relatively difficult and hard to manage. Once we reach a certain point in life, complete simplification—with rare exceptions—is no longer possible. Ironically, this fact is something for which we can be partially thankful. Rather than lament the multitude of worries with which we are confronted, as unwelcome and as painful as those worries can be, we can be thankful for these challenges, as they strip away our false sense of self-sufficiency and force us to grow in faith.

A complicated life, with all of its chaos and concerns, typically feels out of control—and we do not like being out of control. In reality, however, control was never ours to begin with, and the chaos in our lives can help us recognize that fact. It is only our self-delusion during calmer moments that lets us imagine we are in control, and it is during those times of delusion that our recognition of our dependency on God fades. Chaos, therefore—as unwelcome as it is—ironically comes to our aid, showing us that which always has been the case: our lives are, and have always been, in God's hands, not in ours.

In my own context, when there are too many worries and my life feels out of control, I am driven to prayer out of pure necessity, because prayer—which ideally should be the first and best approach to any of my concerns anyway—becomes my only remaining alternative to a life of anxiety or despair. And such prayers should not only—or even primarily—be prayers of request, but more importantly should be prayers of trust, of yielding to God's providence and timing. We have two choices: We trust our worries to God, or we fester over our worries. The former brings peace and strength. The latter beats us down. I hate chaos ... but I love that I can trust in God. I am *not* thankful for the complexity of my life ... but I *am* thankful for what that complexity forces me to do.

I will—and should—always strive to keep my life from becoming unmanageable and out of control, but I know that such a goal is not always possible. I want to lead a life of gratitude, and I want to grow in faith, but I need help with both of these goals. In the end I believe we *should* work hard against the invasion of chaos and excess complexity in life. Nevertheless, given that we will never fully succeed in that endeavor, at least we can be grateful that the inevitable presence of chaos in our lives strips us of our naive sense of self-sufficiency, forces us to trust our Father regarding issues that are beyond our control, and drives us to our knees where we thankfully belong ... and where we should long to be thankful.

30

Bone Marrow

"Will it hurt?" Ian asked. [16]

Ian was a boy not yet ten years old who was about to undergo surgery. His younger sister had a particular cancer of the blood that required a bone marrow transplant, which, especially in those earlier days of its development, was a dangerous and complex procedure. In a bone marrow transplant the cancer patient—in this case, Ian's sister—would receive powerful chemotherapy and whole-body radiation therapy in order to completely destroy not only all of the blood cells in her blood vessels, but also all of the blood-producing cells in her bone marrow. Although the total volume of her blood would not change, every cell in her blood stream and bone marrow would be dead, both the healthy and the cancerous blood cells. Those were the days before healthy stem cells could be used from a patient's own blood system, so the only option for Ian's sister would be to receive a small volume of bone marrow donated

---

[16] This is not a story that I personally witnessed. It happened before I started working at this particular hospital, but the story was told to me by those who were there. Because it is such a moving story, I am taking liberties and including it here.

by someone else (a "donor"). This new donated bone marrow would establish itself in her bone marrow, taking over the job of producing all of her blood cells, but now without her blood cancer—those cancer cells would have all been already killed by the chemotherapy and radiation therapy. The step of destroying her entire blood system was irreversible, so it was never done until a compatible donor could be found. Donors, however, were always hard to find, as they needed to have blood that was genetically almost identical to the cancer patient's blood type. Such donors were often family members, as they shared the closest genetics, but even family members often were not compatible donors. Ian's sister was fortunate—Ian was compatible, and he would be giving her a chance at survival.

The physical part of this whole process was not difficult. After the induction of anesthesia, a small hole would be drilled into the donor's bone, a fairly large needle would be inserted into the donor's bone marrow within that bone, and a small amount of bone marrow would be suctioned into the syringe. None of this portion of the transplant process was dangerous, so a donor faced very little risk and usually only had a sore spot in one of his or her bones for a while afterward. Essentially all of the risk was to the cancer patient. After some preparation, this bone marrow sample would be slowly infused into the cancer patient's veins. It would, in accord with its own nature, eventually set up shop in the recipient patient's bone marrow and start going to work, producing an entirely new blood system—a truly amazing process and a major breakthrough in cancer treatment.

As mentioned, Ian was the ideal donor for his younger sister. At the children's hospital an entire treatment team had been developed to help families through this dangerous and scary procedure: specialty physicians, primary care physicians, nurses, psychologists, social workers, religious leaders, among others. As is appropriate, and to the hospital's credit, these patients and their families received lots of support. Regarding Ian, who was too young to understand much of the whole undertaking, the physicians and other staff members did their best to describe the process, including what it physically would entail and how it might help his sister not die of her cancer. After listening and asking various questions, Ian asked if he could have a few moments to walk around and think about it. This request, of course, was instantly granted. After a short while he came back and indicated that he would do it, and everyone thanked him and gave him encouragement.

A short time later the nursing staff were bustling around the procedure room preparing Ian for the procedure. At some point he asked, "Will it hurt?" Someone in the room, thinking he was referring to an aspect of the procedure, asked in return, "Will what hurt?"

"Will it hurt," Ian said, "when I die?"

Everyone froze. There was not a dry eye in the room. Hearing all of the talk about the importance of bone marrow for survival, Ian, at such a tender young age, mistakenly thought that donating some of his bone marrow to his sister meant giving up his life for hers. He, of course, would not die, but he did not know that. In his mind, it was a done deal.

I daresay, Ian outdoes most of us.

Put yourself in Ian's shoes. Five minutes before he was first presented with this opportunity to help his sister, he had no warning of what would be asked of him. At ten years old he was cruising along in life as always, and then, to his understanding, in the blink of an eye he was being asked to give it all up—a request that was far beyond his maturity level. Would you and I have been similarly ready? *Are you and I now ready?* And ready to give up our lives or something else in a way that likewise might be far beyond our own maturity level?

In my prayers I sometimes reflect on Ian, as I do not want to be taken unprepared if one day I am asked to do what he did, albeit undoubtedly in a different fashion. Such things do happen in life. I know myself to be cowardly enough that I might balk at such an opportunity, so I want to keep my heart ready for it, as it is not an opportunity that typically presents itself with much warning, or in a fashion that I would probably like. Of course, I do not overly dwell on the issue of dying, as that would be morbid, but I also do not shy away from it.

After all, one day God might call me to be Ian.

31

That's Who?

"But, Doc, that's me!"

Dmitri said it with a shy smile, a soft voice, a slight shrug of the shoulders, and no ill intent. He simply was being honest, and honesty is something any physician appreciates—whether or not we agree with the patient. Honesty, at least, is a starting point for change.

His wife was not so appreciative.

In his early twenties, Dmitri had been married for several years. Demonstratively friendly, he made for charming and delightful company, and I always enjoyed his clinic visits. Dmitri was the kind of person one would fondly call "a character," and he liked being that way, as it represented his fundamental personality and his approach to life, and it tended to make others happy around him.

His struggles arose at home, where it was safe to let his less-admirable qualities show forth. He would come home from the stresses at his job needing to unwind, and his fiery temper could flare unpredictably. Never once did he lay a finger on his wife—Dmitri made that point clear—but his walls, doors, and sometimes even furniture were not so lucky. Often there were holes in the wall that he later had to patch up. Verbally his wife did not escape so easily either, as Dmitri often would become loud in his arguments with her. His anger could ignite in an instant, sometimes even before he knew why he became so worked up.

This type of anger is sometimes called "precognitive" (meaning "before one thinks about it"), wherein a patient loses his temper as a *reflex* to some trigger rather than as a consequence of one's thoughts about that trigger. I have had numerous patients describe this phenomenon, but Jane—one of the nicest patients I know—gave a particularly apt example: She was talking with her boss calmly at work one day, and her boss said something that struck Jane the wrong way. Jane's temper instantly flared *before* she could think it through, and she began yelling at her boss. About two to three seconds later, when the thinking part of her brain caught up and processed what her boss had said, Jane realized that she was horribly overreacting—her boss's comment actually was not that big a deal—but it was too late. Jane's tirade was pouring forth, and her boss's eyes were getting bigger every second. Jane told me that she literally watched herself spewing anger, while she desperately tried to stop but was unable to do so, all the while thinking, "You idiot! Stop! You are horribly overreacting! You are going to lose your job for sure!" And lose it she did.

Such was Dmitri's temper. When I described the phenomenon of precognitive anger, the heads of Dmitri and his wife vigorously nodded—that was him! The three of us were in the clinic room together, discussing their marital struggles, and his wife described how distressful home life could be. Dmitri, apologetic to the point of tears, confessed how much he hated hurting his wife's feelings, and he wondered what to do. As I went through the various treatment options, I described how the goal would be to slow down his reflexive anger sufficiently so that he could *think* before blowing up, thereby allowing him to keep his anger in check. His wife looked relieved—and hopeful.

Dmitri balked.

Faced with the possibility that his temper would be different, he sheepishly exclaimed, "But, Doc, that's me!" Dmitri had grown accustomed to his anger, and it therefore had now become a part of his character that he believed partly defined his flamboyant personality. Even if hurtful to his family, he was afraid that the loss of it would transform him into someone he was not, or perhaps better put, into someone he did not want to be. So he preferred not to change. The clinic visit ended without any progress—it was not one of Dmitri's better moments.

It is easy in this story to judge Dmitri, but remember that you and I stare him in the eye every time we look at ourselves in the mirror—all of us are like him in some fashion or another. Each of us has personality traits that are difficult on those around us. None of us is exempt. These traits make up some of who we are, or at least some of whom we *think* we are, and to lose them would feel like becoming someone else. Or perhaps, alternatively, we have grown accustomed to those traits, sometimes liking or even treasuring them. So we hold onto them.

We all must be willing to confront this uncomfortable issue and to let go of any aspect of our personality that serves ourselves and does not serve others. And although that process starts and ends with prayer—prayer for humility, and for the strength to face our imperfections and grow away from them—this is one form of prayer that typically is less effective without the helpful input of those who love us.

Such input is not always a pleasure to receive.

I have many imperfections in my character that burden other people, and unfortunately, most of those flaws are invisible to me ... but they are readily visible to my family and friends. And when—with gentle or not-so-gentle words—these imperfections are first pointed out to me, or when I simply recognize such flaws through the ill fruits of my behavior, for a variety of reasons I bristle at the information. Later on during prayer, after I have had time to adjust and when I feel less emotionally threatened, I know deep down that I cannot pretend to be in the presence of God and yet ignore those blemishes. So I am forced to face myself—uncomfortable though that might be. I try to pray about what I was taught regarding my character, asking God to help me work it through and change for the better. Humility can be difficult(!), and I am no better at it than anyone else. But do I really want to hold onto that unhelpful part of my personality with which I have grown comfortable? Or do I want to let that part of me go and thereby better serve others ... and be happier in the process?

By all of this I do not mean that we must give up our personalities and become someone completely different. Dmitri's mistake was to think that receiving help to control his temper would alter his personality for the worse rather than for the better, or that he would lose a precious part of himself. In truth, he readily could have left his anger behind and still been the passionate character that I loved and admired, manifesting his flamboyant personality in a way that served his wife rather than threatened her. To his credit, Dmitri did do that very thing during his next clinic visit, changing his mind and starting treatment that helped him keep his temper in check—a turnabout that made both him and his wife happy for the next several years that I cared for them. I lost touch with Dmitri when he moved out of state years ago, but I hope and presume that his newfound happiness and priorities have never changed.

Do you and I say, "But, Doc, that's me!" when our Great Physician tries to help us change our hearts for the better? Eventually, at the end of our lives, we will have to leave those parts of our personalities behind anyway, as they will not fit into heaven. In the meantime, if we want to lead a more godly life here and now, we have neither the strength nor the wisdom to accomplish that task on our own. We must be open to the input of our loved ones around us, and we should ask our Physician for help. He always has the perfect treatments ready at hand.

And He is happy to oblige.

32

Sin

John had high blood pressure, high cholesterol, diabetes, and heart disease. He *loved* french fries, one of the worst things he could eat given his medical diagnoses, but it was one of his "feel good" foods. Traveling a lot, often with limited time and minimal access to healthy food, John often found himself grabbing a quick meal at fast food restaurants. As you can imagine, temptation eagerly presented itself at each opportunity. His resistance to the "forbidden fruit" was heartfelt, but he often caved in and splurged, as you and I also likely would do. When back in clinic, despite my reassurances and encouragement, he felt guilty and embarrassed, and he would avert his eyes when confessing his "failures" to me.

John's problem was *not* that his no to french fries was too weak (all of our noes are too weak!), but that he did not have a yes to something better. Although there are a multitude of reasons why temptations occur, many temptations are simply trying to fill voids in our lives. Absent a void, many temptations would not be tempting. Think about it: If you have eaten so much food that you are stuffed, does a forbidden dessert have more than a token ability to tempt you? Or during the happiest moment you can remember with someone you love, did you have any struggle in resisting a less-desirable competing activity? Whatever voids those temptations were trying to fill in your life would already be full. Temptation would lose its power.

The problem comes when we have nothing positive to satisfy our voids, in which case temptations happily try to fill that niche. Worse yet, resisting a temptation without filling the void with something positive makes the void by contrast *feel* bigger, even though in reality it is not. In other words, resisting temptation ironically can increase temptation. It is said that Christians should "resist Satan, but *flee* from temptation."[17] We are advised to flee rather than resist, because resisting temptation by definition means that we remain in the presence of that temptation, and eventually we can be lured into it due to our human weakness.

Reflect on Adam and Eve. Eve's problem in the garden of Eden was not that her no to Satan was not strong enough but that she did not recognize the deep relationship with the Lord that would be lost in the taking of the fruit. She saw her choices as "It looks tasty, and I will know what God knows" versus "I am not supposed to eat of the fruit." Her comparison should have been "It looks tasty, and I will know what God knows" versus "The deep riches of my relationship with God, which I will lose in the taking of the fruit, make those tempting treats look like dried-up dust in comparison."

---

[17] I do not mean that we should not also resist temptation. For *every* temptation there is a need to resist. My point here is that fleeing temptation is always the best option when it is available, especially when it appears that our resistance is weakening or threatened.

My patient John, to his credit, overcame his craving of french fries, but only when he embraced an overall healthy lifestyle. Ignoring the issue of fries in particular, he decided to change his entire diet. He also started exercising, lost weight, and had more energy. John thereby felt better than he had in years. The void of "wanting to feel good" was now full. Junk food as "feel good food" did not sound good to him anymore. In fact, it sounded unattractive. Temptation wasn't very tempting.

A common phrase in competitive sports is "the best defense is a good offense." Translating that perspective into the spiritual realm, your best defense against sin is to promote a strong offense: *deepen your devotion!* In my experience, holiness is 10 percent rejecting sin and 90 percent promoting love of God. When in the presence of God, sin feels as distasteful and undesirable as it truly is in life. Outside of the presence of God, when our physical nature is often dominant, that same sin feels very attractive. Therefore, as I stress above, let your prayers be first and foremost aimed at building relationship with your Lord. Let prayer be to your spiritual life what John's healthy lifestyle was to his physical life: filling your voids to overflowing.

It *is* good to have a strong no to temptation. Indeed, the stronger your no, the better. But saying yes to deep devotion is the best way to avoid sin.

33

Repent or Repeat

Shelly looked at me with her tired, discouraged eyes. I had seen those eyes on her face many times before. Unfortunately over the years her plight had never become easier for me to witness or for her to live out, so at the moment we were both feeling disheartened. Yes, she volunteered, she was back with her abusive boyfriend. Even though I years ago had ceased to ask her "Why?" for the explicit purpose of understanding her reasons, I continued to ask her "Why?" in order to help her work through her struggles, hoping that she might one day take charge of her life and move forward—and away from that destructive relationship. I have been Shelly's physician for many years, and she trusts me deeply. I therefore have been able to probe into her life without causing offense.

Although she knew that her boyfriend was destructive to her, she did not have the strength to leave him and venture out on her own, away from companionship (even harmful companionship can provide a familiar comfort at times) and into the scary world of self-sufficiency and psychological health. Shelly's repeated mantra, expressed to me many times in various words and in different forms, was, "I know I should leave him." It was rarely followed by action. Shelly knew her weaknesses. She was dependent on her boyfriend to fill the emotional voids in her life that she had acquired from a difficult childhood. Even though she could see how he was causing her psychological harm, she could not fix her core beliefs and feelings of inadequacy in order to leave him. It was clear to both of us that Shelly did not have what it took to get herself out of her ditch. She repented to me frequently in words, and sometimes she would leave her boyfriend for a short time, but she always went back. She did not reach beyond herself for the help needed to accomplish what she could not accomplish on her own.

We are all Shelly. Her plight is ours when we repent to God in our prayers about our weaknesses. I am convinced that we all have numerous psychological voids, certain irrational core beliefs about ourselves, and various destructive habits of body or soul that we do not have the power *on our own* to heal or to leave behind. As with Shelly, these failings can lead us into bad choices, big or small. In our prayers, when we are able to admit our personal faults, we often *repent* to God on our knees, but we then *repeat* our bad choices on our feet. As most Christians know, repentance is a three-part process: heartfelt confession of sorrow, restitution for whatever our actions have cost others, and then the determination not to repeat the same errors. This last issue is where we often fail, because our habitual bad choices are usually rooted in our personal failings that I list above, and we are unable to heal those things on our own.

What, then, should we do? The same thing I told Shelly to do: *Get help!* I remember repeatedly telling her to seek support from her family. She refused to do so, not because her family was unwilling to help but because she did not want to change. You and I can be the same. Whether due to pride, a lack of desire to quit our habitual sins, a fear of what others will think if we disclose our embarrassing flaws, or a myriad of other reasons, we often do not seek help. We "go it alone" and thereby remain stuck in our proverbial rut.

When things finally got bad enough, Shelly did seek assistance, and she was able to leave her boyfriend for good. Her life improved, and she was exceedingly glad for it. My question for us is whether *we* want to leave our bad choices behind and whether we are humble enough to seek the help we need from others to make up for our shortcomings. I believe God will provide that help if we are willing to avail ourselves of it. If we are not, then our prayers fall short. We cannot blame God for not delivering us from our repetitive errors if we are not willing to walk on our feet in repentance as hard as we pray on our knees in repentance. We can truly repent, or we can repeat. The choice is ours.

34

Incubation Period

He literally ran from me.

I was working in the emergency room during my residency training, and the next patient to be seen was Grant. Grabbing his medical chart from the rack, I walked over to his exam room and greeted him warmly, introducing myself in the process. Grant was a healthy-appearing young man, in his mid twenties, with dark hair and a medium complexion. He barely returned my greeting and did not smile at all, which was not a rare response from some of the patients at our hospital. But Grant was different ... his terse response was not due to rudeness but to an all-consuming terror. He related to me his concern.

He had a sore throat.

I tried not to show my feelings. Such a medical problem typically is quite simple and benign, so his abject fear seemed out of place, and I was surprised that he looked so deeply concerned over such a small symptom. After further questioning I began the physical exam. Along with an appropriate evaluation of all other relevant organ systems, I looked into Grant's throat—and it did not look good. He had an easily recognizable and very extensive case of oral thrush.[18] For a generally healthy young adult who had not been on a recent course of antibiotics or steroids, the degree of Grant's thrush was worrisome, likely indicating a significant deficiency in the immune system. Through further questioning I found out that Grant had recently arrived in California from New York City, where he had not been a stranger to an active nightlife with women. All of this happened during the early years of the AIDS epidemic before there were any treatments, and New York City was one of the worst cities affected.

Of course, Grant knew all of this as well, but he clearly was hoping against hope that the cause of his sore throat was something more mundane. So when I, with as gentle a voice as possible, suggested that we run various tests including a lab test for HIV, Grant all but panicked, unable to face the possibility of having AIDS, as it was a death sentence in those days. Blurting out, "No! No!" in a broken voice, he bolted from the room past me before I could react. I tried to call him back—although there is very little that a physician can say in the packed corridor of an ER without compromising privacy—but it was to no avail. Grant disappeared around a corner with remarkable speed. I never saw him again. Given the lack of treatments available at the time, I cannot imagine that he lived very long.

One of the most frightening aspects of AIDS is its long incubation period, meaning the time it takes from initial infection with the HIV virus until the first symptoms develop (in more precise medical terminology, the time interval between HIV infection and the development of symptomatic AIDS). At the time of the writing of this book, the best assessment is that this incubation

---

[18] Oral thrush is caused by an overgrowth of yeast in the mouth.

period averages ten years for young men like Grant, although it can range from a few months to twenty years. That means that Grant might have been infected—and spreading the disease to others—but still feeling perfectly well for ten or more years before developing his "sore throat." This incubation period can lead people into complacency about their activities for a long time before the consequences catch up with them ... or tragically affect someone else.

Sin is similar. It can be years before the consequences of our bad choices present themselves. Once starting a sinful habit, however serious it might be, the lack of immediate consequences (what one might call the "symptoms" of our sins) can lull us into a false sense of security that we can get away with it all. "Hey, this is going well" too easily becomes our mantra. But we should not be fooled—it always catches up with us at some point. Sin, similar to deadly virus, does not stay dormant forever. And the consequences of neglected sin can be just as dire, both for us and for the people around us whose lives we might negatively be affecting by our actions and character.

Prayer is not a time only for fellowship with the Lord. Without intending to sound overly negative, I submit that prayer is also a time of reckoning ... and thanks be to God for that! In modern-day medicine there are no cures for some of the infectious ailments we see in clinic, but in God's clinic there is a cure for every spiritual illness that exists—but only if we are open to His reckoning ... and if we pray in the first place. Incubation periods for our souls are a blessing, in that they allow us to pursue healing before it is too late, but such periods also can be deceptively peaceful.

Never be lulled.

35

Past and Future

"I know," he said to me, "the ravings of a fool."

Those were Richard's exact words, but I have heard the same confession in many different forms from men and women alike. Richard had recently committed adultery, contracting a venereal disease as a consequence. His wife, by her own confession, was essentially never physically intimate with Richard, so he spent most of his marriage feeling frustrated and neglected. Because Richard and his wife were still fairly young, it was in truth very difficult on him, and, to his credit, he did try to be patient. Nevertheless, by his own admission, that did not excuse his actions. An opportunity had presented itself, and he found himself pulled into it—an action he now regretted ... a bit too late.

Temptation does an odd thing to us, something we typically do not even recognize at the time, but which is easily visible if we just look for it. And that look just might make all the difference. The next time you are sorely tempted, examine your heart and see if the following occurs.

When temptation is strong, we find that our experience of the current moment—the "now," so to speak—grows very powerful, and our focus telescopes down to that one instant, drowning out our awareness of everything else. And among the "everything else" are two issues of particularly importance: our past and our future. The degree to which this telescoping of our focus happens depends on the magnitude of the temptation at hand, but it occurs every time.

Our *past*, with its commitments, resolutions, oaths, moral values, honor, fidelity, and faith—the issues that define our character—fades away like a distant memory, manifestly too weak in our minds to counter the temptation at hand. Our *future*, with its obligations, goals, destinies, and logical consequences, hides from view as if in an impenetrable fog. And even if we are able to recognize those negative future consequences, they feel trivial in comparison to the seemingly blissful rewards promised by the temptation at hand. The temptation before us therefore becomes the only thing we can see or feel. So there we stand, bereft of the moral anchors of the past and of the natural consequences of the future, in essence abandoned and alone in our fight against the lure of forbidden pleasures. Having a human nature that is weak of will and easy to topple, it is no wonder we lose the battle so often.

Of course, if we do fall to temptation, our past and our future—which were never really gone in the first place—brutally reappear. Better put, they come crashing down upon us. The betrayed commitments of our past accuse us of our failure, and the consequences of our actions now loom threateningly in our future. We exclaim silently to ourselves, "What was I thinking!" The problem, of course, is that we were *not* thinking—we were only feeling.

This loss of our future and of our past is a huge problem. But it also offers a good solution. We face temptations every day of our lives. The question is how we should pray ourselves through those trials.

The easiest answer to that question is how we are *not* to pray: our first and primary prayer should not be simply to resist the temptation. Praying thus is a blunder, because doing so merely keeps our attention focused on the temptation itself. We need our focus to be elsewhere ... but not just anywhere.

Yes, any type of distraction can be helpful, but during temptation the best option is to pray specifically to see our past and our future. *They* will help save us. I personally have found this strategy to be wonderfully practical.

Jesus was successful in remaining sinless partly because, in the midst of temptation, He never lost sight of His past or His future. Look at Hebrews 12: Jesus, for the "joy that was set before Him," endured the cross, scorning its shame. But there certainly was no joy on the cross! Indeed, He once said to His disciples in Luke 12:50f, "I have a baptism with which to be baptized, and what stress I am under until it is completed!" The joy that was set before Him was not the cross itself—a miserable event that He dreaded—but the upcoming fulfillment *after* that suffering. As Jesus entered into the events of the Passion, the temptation to stop the process and avoid the upcoming misery must have been almost overwhelming. Nevertheless, Jesus was able to see from where He originated and why He had come to earth (His past). He likewise never lost sight of the goal beyond the current temptation, to the time after the suffering when He would rise from the dead and the joys of His sacrifice would be realized (His future). His past and His future were crystal clear to Him.

So He endured. We should desire to maintain such perspectives in our lives as well.

We should not make the mistake of trying to accomplish Jesus's feat by our own power. As I mentioned, we are weak of will and do not have the strength on our own to fight off big temptations. Pray! Be aware of Jesus's presence. He really is there at the moment, and it is always harder to succumb to our "secret" sins when someone else is in the room, especially when that someone is our Lord. Jesus also is the only one strong enough to bring us back to our senses when our resolve is at risk.

Temptation is a very practical assailant, and we need practical solutions. Next time you find yourself under attack, turn your heart to Jesus and pray for Him to restore your past and your future.

They never really left.

36

Hostage?

"You're holding my medications hostage!"

So thought Larry, and he was not pleased about it. In his sixties, Larry was overall fairly healthy but with a few medical problems such as high blood pressure and some mildly arthritic joints. It had been over one year since he had last seen me, so Larry therefore was overdue for a clinic visit to make sure he was— and would remain—healthy. It is considered standard of care in medicine that such follow-up visits be routinely scheduled, but the frequency of such clinic appointments depends on many factors, such as the patient's age, the severity and number of illnesses, the types and quantity of medications taken, whether the patient has been recently hospitalized, etc. For patients with multiple complex medical problems, we like to see them every few weeks to months. For patients in overall good health but who take medications for stable medical conditions, we might see them once or twice a year, but never less than every twelve months, especially for the elderly. These follow-up visits are considered essential, as they involve several crucially important objectives: discussion of overall health, anticipation of potential future illnesses, plans on how to avoid unhealthy pitfalls, effectiveness or possible side effects of medications, any new or worrisome symptoms, a physical exam, surveillance lab tests, possibly x-rays, etc. And this list barely scratches the surface. If one of my patients takes daily prescription medications and has not seen me for too long, my office staff has been taught to schedule him or her for a follow-up appointment as a requirement for further medication refills.[19] Such was the case with Larry.

He was not happy.

I knew Larry and his wife well, having been their physician for many years, and, from my perspective, we had a close personal relationship. I was therefore surprised when my staff told me that he objected to having to come in, so I called him to find out what the problem might be. Sensing only frustration in his voice, I heard him say that he felt fine, did not have any questions or concerns, that his home blood pressures were normal (to his credit, he measured his blood pressures at home as I had suggested), and that I was holding his medications hostage just to "force" him to come in. When I tried to explain that there are many important reasons to come in for periodic maintenance evaluations beyond just the issue of high blood pressure, he did not budge. He said he felt fine, reiterated that I was holding his medications hostage, and asserted that the visit was unnecessary. He wanted and expected me simply to refill his medications. That, of course, I could not do, as such an action would represent terribly deficient—not to mention heartless—medical care. It would be unconscionable to prescribe medications year after year, not taking care of Larry until some complication or potentially fatal but preventable illness drove

---

[19] Abruptly stopping medications can be dangerous. Therefore, as is logical and as would be expected, we provide our patients with refills until they are able to come in for their appointment.

him back into my clinic. Physicians *care* for patients; we do not simply act as medication dispensaries.

Part of Larry's misunderstanding was thinking that because he *felt* fine, he therefore *was* fine. In reality, his blood pressure condition was only a tiny part of what would be dealt with at the visit. As important as, or perhaps even more important than, his blood pressure would be the many other reasons for the appointment, such as I listed in the first paragraph above. In the silence of our thoughts, we physicians very quickly leaf through an incredible number of potential concerns while a patient is in the room, thoughts that the patient never sees simply because it would take hours to explain it all—and even if we tried to do so, the explanation would be inadequate and would, in the end, leave the patient with information overload and would cause confusion, not clarity. While I personally believe that patients should be aggressively educated so that they can actively take charge of their health—I often fall behind on my daily schedule because of the time I spend teaching my patients—a *comprehensive* discussion of every possible theoretical medical concern would be impractical and even counterproductive. One simply cannot condense seven or more years of medical training and thirty years of clinical experience into such a conversation.

Health is a tricky business, with innumerable potential pitfalls and wrong turns to avoid, as well as future problems either to prevent when possible or discover early when not. It is unrealistic to expect a patient to know all, or even most, of those concerns. There is consequently an unavoidable level of trust that must be present between the patient and doctor, trust that the doctor is conscientiously keeping track of current problems and trying to avoid future ones. That is, after all, our privileged role.

In the same way that I expected Larry—for his sake, not for mine—to see me for periodic evaluations, God expects you and me to visit Him, our Great Physician, regularly in prayer. Rather than being legalistic or over-demanding, this expectation is a blessing. When we neglect Him, especially for long periods of time, is it to His detriment, or to ours? Does He suffer harm, or do we? Unfortunately, most of us too easily consider prayer a bother, as it cuts into our daily schedule or preferred activities. I certainly have fallen into that trap. Then we expect God to give us the things we want anyway, admittedly without really knowing whether those things are good for us—after all, we never stopped and bothered to ask Him if they are.

If one considers prayer as a duty—or merely as a time to talk to God, or to ask Him for things, or just an opportunity to tell Him about our day—then it is somewhat understandable why we balk at having to pray on a regular basis. But if prayer is understood primarily as a time to deepen our love of Him, then it becomes clear why He expects us to spend consistent time on our knees. One cannot expect to fall in love without regular quality time together. And it is His *presence*, above all else, that He longs to give us—even more than He wants to give us individual blessings in life. So I believe that God, for our sake, holds back on certain blessings when we neglect Him, not because He is legalistic or petty, but for two other good reasons: first, the lack of those blessings can make us wake up and sense our need of Him again; and second, in the same way that Larry's medications (a medical blessing for his health, given the devastating medical consequences of untreated high blood pressure) might cause silent side effects if not carefully monitored, our blessings from God, if our hearts are not spiritually guided and monitored by our Physician, might cause spiritual "side effects." For example, as our hearts drift away from Him due to lack of prayer—allowing us perhaps to become egocentric or to lose humility—we might perceive God's blessings as deserved, or as things we believe are owed to us, or as evidence of our own self-importance, leading us to become spoiled or arrogant rather than remaining humble and receiving those blessings as the gifts from God that they truly are.

In the same way that Larry only knew a small fraction of the concerns and evaluations that would go through my mind during his visit with me, you and I know only a tiny percentage of what God aims to teach us when we have our visits with Him in prayer. He knows what we need, and we generally do not. He sees tomorrow, and we *certainly* do not. So the only good option is to trust that His requirements of consistent prayer truly are necessary and are "healthy" for us.

From our worldly perspective, we tend to want God's blessings but not His requirements. When we are in our right minds—on God's level, so to speak—we will want His requirements first, because only then will His blessings remain a blessing.

37

✦

Ossify?

I have spent countless hours among the elderly in nursing homes and in my clinic. One of the most consistent patterns I have witnessed is the habit of many people—although certainly not all!—to "ossify" into their lifestyles as they grow old. The word *ossify* is derived from the Latin word for bone, and when used to describe someone's personality, it means to become like bone: hard, unyielding, inflexible, unchanging ... to become "set in one's ways." This tendency is hard to resist, and if left to our own devices, we all naturally evolve that way as we age if we become too comfortable in life. If such an evolution happens, the question is not *whether* you and I will ossify over time but rather *into what* we will ossify. If we are careless and do not let God continue to be active in our lives, we will drift toward greater self-absorption and protection of our interests, and once ossified, we might not even recognize our stubborn intransigence or our self-centered perspectives. None of us should think we are immune to such a fate.

It is therefore a gift of God to keep us uncomfortable in our lives as we grow older, as that keeps us permanently flexible. I have always loved (and hated!) the prayer a pastor taught me when I was in medical school: "Lord, comfort the broken, and break the comfortable." As I advance in years, I can feel myself more and more drawn toward comfort and complacency. I want to curl up in front of a fire with a nice book and let the world's problems swirl around me at a safe distance, while I keep those problems and demands *outside* of my ever-shrinking domain. This trend, if left unchecked, inevitably leads to spiritual laziness—when we are too comfortable we no longer need God, and we no longer are of much use to others. Comfort slowly becomes smugness, which, if we are not careful, in turn leads to arrogance, presumption, and lack of empathy. Lord, save me from such a fate! When in my right mind, I do not want to live out such a scenario, but it can be a difficult temptation to fight.

The more comfortable we become, the more that comfort becomes a favored treasure, and because by nature we humans try to protect that which we treasure, our comfort then becomes something to be defended: we put up stone walls and a moat to ward off any disruption of our peace and quiet. We start to resent intrusions and to become less vigilant to the needs of those around us. Self-centeredness thereafter becomes unavoidable—a development that God certainly does not want for us. Reflect on the New Testament church, which became too comfortable in Jerusalem during the first years of the church, not taking to heart Jesus's command to "go unto all nations." God brought the Romans in the year AD 72 and scattered the church to the winds. That was not an easy time for God's people, but it was necessary both for their growth (not to mention their joy!) and for God's plan for human history.

Prayer is always to be practiced with this risk in mind. We should enter prayer with openness—actively desiring His *disruptive* leadership—and we should never expect to remain complacent, because our Lord, whose instructions can be quite creative, has our infinite happiness, not our comfort, at heart. Whether His bidding comes immediately during prayer or later on through life experiences, He is very unpredictable.

Be ready for anything.

38

Better or Bitter?

"Take it from me, Doc—it's no fun getting old!"

And he was right. I have heard aging described—somewhat cynically, but not altogether off the mark—as a series of losses: loss of health, loss of friends, loss of independence, loss of family, loss of energy, loss of mobility, and so forth. No matter one's view of life, such things truly are "no fun." As time passes and the body winds down, things that once made us happy simply start to go, and the process is unstoppable. I hear it from my elderly patients on a frequent basis. I also see it visibly in their lives as I care for them over the decades.

But there is an optimistic flip side to that coin, something I witness around me in worship every week, and it far outweighs the pessimistic side of the coin. The elderly in church are such an encouragement to me, more than I can describe, and I love sitting next to them in the pews. They often have such a singular focus on the Lord, as they have less to distract them in mind and body.

As the body slows down and all of the above-mentioned losses pile up, our focus on God can improve ... *if* we do not allow ourselves to become bitter. I always have loved and laughed at Mark Twain's quote, "Youth is wasted on the young." It is such a clever phrase. Yet, even though the quote *feels* so true, it is subtly misleading, because its premise is that "youth" is such a treasure. Yes, it is wonderful to feel young, healthy, and carefree, but most young people have so little sense of their mortality. Their lives can feel so full of possibilities, a seemingly endless future, boundless energy, and untroubled play. But such a life does not suit a wizened elder. Even I, merely in my fifties, do not want such a life again. The "treasure" of feeling young again is not the treasure it pretends to be. Although there are exceptions, the elderly I see in church each week, especially the ones who come early to pray, have hearts that are preparing to see their Lord sooner rather than later. No longer in love with their bodies, knowing their futures to be short, and no longer seeking to be important in the eyes of people around them, they can be freed up to concentrate on the primary relationship for which they were created—love of God.

We are sojourners here on earth, and our allotted time is like the blink of an eye. For the most part, the losses of aging (I am *not* referring here to the loss of loved ones such as friends and family!) are partly the means by which God strips us of our addiction to worldly pleasures. Those pleasures, although not bad in and of themselves, can distract us or pull us away from the far greater treasures that God brings to our lives. Over time, it is a blessing, not a curse, to lose our attachments to the material attractions of this world. In my own life I have found that as I age, I pray more. I long for heaven more. I better recognize worldly pleasures for what they really are: nice to have, but superficial fluff compared with the sumptuous feast

R. Keith McAfee, Jr, MD

being prepared for us. Therefore, as my losses pile up, my gains pile up more. As my prayers become more and more surrounded by my aging life, they become better ...

... not bitter.

39

They Can?

"Yes he does!"

And she believed every word of it. Her face showed absolute conviction, and her eyes conveyed an honest, sincere bafflement that I could even question the fact. I had known Dani since she was very young, and by now she had become an attractive teenager of fourteen years old. Her mother, in the clinic room with us, mentioned with as neutral a voice as she could muster that Dani had had sex for the first time the past weekend. Many teenagers would have looked defiant at a moment like this, but Dani simply looked proud. In her eyes, she was entering the adult world with its adult "privileges," and she was pleased with herself. She also thought her guy was beyond reproach.

Her guy in actuality was a young man several years older than Dani who had another steady girlfriend at the time, and he simply was cheating on his girlfriend and was using Dani for his enjoyment. Knowing this development for what it really was, I was sad for Dani, whom I knew well and for whom I cared deeply. Although I did not show it on the outside, inwardly I ached that she had fallen prey to the manipulative voyeurism of a man who regarded her merely as a tool for his pleasure, later to be discarded (which, of course, is eventually what happened). After discussing some medical questions that were of concern to Dani and to her mother, I examined Dani's abdomen, looked at her kindly, and asked with a gentle voice, "You do know that he does not really love you, right?" Hence her incredulous look and her three fateful words, "Yes he does!" The man's silvery tongue had done its job well.

Dani, unfortunately, represents us all. However, your and my naïve vulnerability is toward the pleasures of this world: material goods, power, popularity, wealth, etc. Satan, with his silvery tongue, promises happiness when we seek after such things. We really should know better, but when we are warned that these things cannot fulfill us, we all too often—through our actions more often than through our words—blurt out with conviction, "Yes they can!" The amazing and tragic truth about Dani's response to me was not her blindness to her "boyfriend's" deception, but her *blindness to her blindness*. She so badly wanted to believe that she was loved, that she bought his ploy without reservation. In relation to the false promises of this material world, you and I do the same.

The dilemma is how to get out of that trap, that blindness to our blindness. By definition, when we are in that state we do not know it—we are blind to it. Worse yet, not only are we blind to it, but we typically have little motivation to become unblinded, because in some fashion we enjoy whatever has seduced us, leaving us not wanting to give up that pleasure. This pitfall presents us with a double dilemma: blind, and liking it that way. Never underestimate this trap, as we are all woefully vulnerable to it.

Our only hope, then, is to be told about it ... and the news must come from outside of us. That is never a welcomed event! Someone, be it another person or God Himself, has to be the bearer of bad news—undoubtedly news that we will not want to hear. I do not know anyone who responds favorably to such information. In truth, the person who tells us is the one person who cares for us most, or he or she would not risk offending us. We should not shun that person: he or she might be our salvation.[20] If that person is God, then He will let us know through our conscience, or through unwelcome experiences that will point out our addiction. But whether another person or God, I submit that we, on our own, never have hearts that are naturally ready to be told that we are blind or addicted.

This is where prayer comes into play. We simply *must* make it a regular part of our prayer life to ask for the strength and openness to be ready—at any time—to face this unwelcomed news. We need God to change our perspective from *not* wanting to hear it, to wanting desperately to hear it, which is a difficult transition. Wanting to be informed of our flaws is our only hope. Remember that addictions do not just cause harm; they *kill*. This brutal, cold, hard fact of life is something I have witnessed in my patients too often, many times consoling family members left behind when the patient dies. Physical addictions can kill our bodies, behavioral addictions can kill our relationships, and spiritual addictions can kill our souls. These are not trivial consequences.

---

[20] I also want to emphasize here that we should not run around judging other people and looking for ways to tell them about some aspect of their lives that should be improved. That role is a delicate one and should be left to other people's families, pastors/priests, and very closest of friends.

I believe that every one of us, without exception, will face the dilemma described above several times in our lives. It is never easy to do so. Our first and most natural inclination will be denial, typically followed in short order by anger or offense. It is, after all, a humiliating experience. I know this not only through seeing it in my medical clinic when I am tactful but forthright with my addicted patients, but also from my own personal life when my own flaws have been pointed out, and I am no better at hearing this news than anyone else. We must *expect* to suffer this humiliation, as it is going to happen to us one way or another. And ironically, the more we resist it, the worse the humiliation will become. I am not trying to sound pessimistic here—just realistic.

It also is true that praying for humility is extremely hard to do when we are in the midst of a humiliating event. The best time to pray for humility is *before* the event. As any athlete will tell us, it is always best to work on good physical conditioning before a competition, not during. We therefore should make it a part of our prayers to acknowledge that we are likely blind about some worldly pleasures that have seduced us, but that we want God to deliver us from those addictions. At times, our Great Physician might be gently asking us the same question that I asked of Dani: "You do know that worldly promises cannot really fulfill you, don't you?"

Let us strive never to answer, "Yes, they can!"

40

As We Forgive Those …

"I am my own worst enemy!" she said with an embarrassed expression.

Primary care physicians hear that sentence frequently, although it is expressed in many forms. On occasion I hear those exact words, but most patients, for various reasons, convey the same meaning more indirectly. And each time I receive that confession, I nod my head in sympathy, provide practical ways to fix the problem, try to be supportive … and I personally empathize. It is surprisingly easy for me not to be judgmental, because, after all, those patients also speak for me—in terms of my spiritual health I am my own worst enemy no less than my patients are regarding their own physical health. In that fact I suspect I am not alone.

No one forces me to choose selfishly, or to prioritize materialism above spiritual growth, or to neglect my Father in prayer, or to do any number of such things. Only *I* can take the unhappy credit for those choices. Like my patients regarding their medical woes, I am surprised at how easily I fall into the same traps over and over, and I get angry with myself for my failings … but perhaps too angry.

Each of us knows the line in the Lord's Prayer, "Forgive us our trespasses, as we forgive those who trespass against us." Because of the order in which those words are arranged, we naturally tend to think of forgiving others when we recite that phrase, but in reality *we* are the ones who do more "trespassing against us" than anyone else. We, not others, are the ones who make the unwise choices in our lives, to the detriment of our hearts, our minds, our relationships, and our faith. Much of the time, it is ourselves, not someone else, whom we must forgive. Speaking for myself, for several reasons I find that hard to do. First of all, I would prefer to ignore the uncomfortable truth that I so often need to be forgiven. Second, honest self-assessment, which is indispensable to the process of forgiving myself, is not something that comes naturally to me—I would avoid it if not pushed by God to do it. Third, because I repeatedly stumble into the same pitfalls despite knowing better than to do so, I often do not think I deserve forgiveness.

Yet forgiveness is never deserved. Such is its nature. In fact, forgiveness is fundamentally unfair—I dare say, *unjust*—in that the wrong person is paying the price, and the guilty party seems to be getting away with something. That is one of the many reasons why forgiveness is such a difficult virtue to practice in general and why we find it so hard to forgive ourselves. Why should we let ourselves off the hook for actions or attitudes that we know we could (and should!) avoid?

I believe there are two major truths that allow us to more easily forgive ourselves. First, for our sake God expects it of us. Forgiving oneself is absolutely necessary for spiritual growth, and refusing to do so leaves us in a stagnant devotional rut. God wants us to move beyond our sins, not wallow in them. Second, I think that most of us—what I call the rank and file Christians who genuinely desire to be good—commit the majority of our sins out of human weakness rather than out of evil motives. That is not to say that bad motives are not part of all of our sins, but I consider our weak will to be the biggest culprit of our failings, and I submit that it is easier to forgive ourselves when we can recognize this truth.

Admittedly, there is an inherent danger in self-forgiveness, in that we could, if we wanted, simply excuse away all of our failings without due repentance and examination of conscience. Such an attitude would be a grave error, but for believers who are at least minimally honest in their self-view, I do not believe it is hard to figure out when we are making that mistake.

In terms of their physical bodies, my patients cannot effectively turn their lives around and take a proactive approach to becoming healthy *until* they leave behind and move beyond their self-condemnation. Regarding our spiritual health, you and I are the same.

41

No, Even So

It was during medical school, and I was having another friendly private discussion of faith with one of my fellow medical students, Mia. She was sharing her views as an atheist, and I was sharing my views as a Christian. Mia was one of my favorite fellow students, and we were able to talk about our different viewpoints frankly but with mutual respect and friendliness. It was wonderful! Neither of us was convinced by the other's arguments, but we were able to hear each other with genuine interest, neither feeling threatened by the other. Toward the end of one particular discussion I asked Mia what for me is one of the most important—if not *the* most important—questions of truth-seeking: If she found out she was wrong, would she change her mind? If through logic she became genuinely convinced of the truth of the gospel, would she follow? Whatever one's beliefs—Christian, atheist, or otherwise—a genuine seeker of truth *must* be able to confront that question and answer in the affirmative. Mia thought for a few moments, and then, with courage and honesty, she admitted that she would not. She confessed that she did not want to give up control of her life, even if she found out that she was wrong about her atheism. And whereas she had been animated and content during our discussion up to that point, she became somewhat more subdued after she made that confession. She realized that she was not the seeker of truth that she claimed to be, because she was not willing to follow wherever truth might lead. Truth took a backseat to control. Even if she was correct as an atheist and I was wrong as a Christian, her quest was not honest.

Unfortunately, my part in the above scenario does not end there. As I pray for Mia, I also pray for myself. Perhaps you might be praying for yourself here as well. When I am able to muster up Mia's courage, I confess that I also sometimes put control of my life in the driver's seat and leave truth in the backseat. Every day in one way or another I take another bite out of the fruit of the garden of Eden, rejecting God's lordship for my own. To avoid hypocrisy, I, like Mia, must confront that same dreaded question: Am I willing to change my lifestyle, my views on a whole host of issues (moral, political, ethical, etc.), my "whatever" when I find I am wrong? I wish it were not so hard to answer yes to that question.

42

War

He took one look at me, backed up quickly, and closed the door. I was once again alone.

This is not a happy story.

The door mentioned above led to a housekeeping utility closet that contained brooms, mops, a full array of cleaning supplies ... and me. A few moments before, I had been standing in the hallway of the inpatient pediatric wing in our training hospital and was told that one of my patients, a beautiful, healthy, giggling 4-month old infant girl whom I had seen the day before for a "well child" clinic visit, had been beaten to death by her amphetamine-intoxicated parents. Starting to lose my composure but not having an easy escape from the open hallway of the pediatric ward, I looked around at my immediate surroundings, spotted the utility closet door, and quickly slipped inside, closing the door behind me. Assuming that I would be alone for a while, I sat on the floor, hugged my legs with my head on my knees, and sobbed. As ill timing would have it, in short order a young janitor, intent on expedient efficiency, burst through the door in pursuit of a cleaning item from the closet. Instead, he found me. Freezing midstride in total confusion, he gaped at my tear-streaked face and within seconds, backed up quickly and left. I continued to cry.

At the manslaughter trial, a separate attorney had been assigned to each spouse. With no other witnesses to the crime other than the parents, a charge of first-degree murder would be impossible to prove unless one of the spouses confessed—something neither of them was about to do. Hence, although both of them certainly were guilty, the couple could only be charged with manslaughter. The best legal strategy was for each spouse to hire a lawyer whose goal would be to try and prove that the *other* spouse was the guilty party. Sitting on the stand during my expert witness testimony, questioned by each attorney in turn, I witnessed a bizarre proceeding in which husband and wife—each having given their vows on their wedding day to a life of mutual fidelity and love—tried to convict the other of murdering their shared child.

As was expected, both parents were found guilty. They were parted and sent to separate prisons for a considerable amount of time. I went back to my residency training, and the child was gone. As I mentioned above, this is not a happy story.

But it is an important one.

In my view, this story epitomizes evil—because evil works that way, with Satan twisting human desires and actions to everyone's detriment. God rewards His faithful followers with joy; Satan rewards his faithful followers with suffering and destruction. We can be certain that the young couple did not grow up wanting this kind of an outcome in life. Years before this event, their initial experimentation with drugs was in all likelihood simply an attempt to get pleasure and have fun, albeit on their own terms. But the pleasure they sought, as is true whenever people choose pleasure over goodness, eventually became their master and led them to this place of misery. Every positive aspect of their lives was destroyed in the process. Their marriage and childrearing turned into a nightmare, such that the committed couple destroyed their own baby and then turned on each other, ultimately leading to their imprisoned isolation and causing them to lose everything of value, including their futures. That is how Satan works: twist and manipulate people to do his evil deeds and then reward those people by destroying their lives as well.

It is against such a foe that we pray. This is no simple game of chess between opposing players. It is war. And the stakes are high. In these chapters I have commented at length about the joys of prayer and about the need for trust, love of God, pursuit of His presence, self-reflection, honesty, and such things. But prayer is also warfare. Our foe is neither fair nor honorable, but is hideous and brutal, doing things that are detestable beyond words. Satan is frighteningly intelligent as well as subtle and insidious in his work, and we stand no chance against him on our own. Left to our own devices, Satan dances circles around us. We can—and should—work with all our strength to thwart and counteract Satan's intents on earth, but we also should not fool ourselves into thinking our work is the deciding factor in these battles.

It is prayer that ultimately wins the war.

Wars are long and difficult affairs. Patience, endurance, and persistence are indispensable. I am thankful that the eventual final outcome is already assured, but you and I are not yet at that end. It is good for us to remember tragedies such as I describe above, as that memory galvanizes our resolve. We are, after all, still on the battlefield. So we fight and work for God's goodness, but more importantly we pray ...

... and the more, the better.

43

Outside the Door

She simply had to endure.

That was how Maria described it to me. Now in her sixties, she still found it hard to maintain her poise as we talked about her early motherhood. Her son Andre, grown up by the time we met Maria, has "classic autism" (also known as Kanner autism)— the most significantly affected form of autism, in which a person often has little or no verbal communication, exhibits limited social interaction, and seems to be in his own world. Several decades ago classic autism was the only recognized form of the disability, but we now realize that autism presents itself in many different degrees of involvement. However, the higher-functioning forms would not be understood or widely recognized until the 1980s and 1990s, decades after Maria's son had grown up.

During Andre's younger years the cause of autism was a mystery, but one of the prevailing opinions was that the mothers were to blame. Mothers of autistic children often were called "refrigerator moms"—pleasant and seemingly caring on the outside, but with an icy and inhospitable personality on the inside. An autistic child's severe social disabilities were thought to be due to a mother who, in the privacy and secrecy of her home, denied her child any relational warmth and maternal nurturing. In public she would play the role of a good mom, but that was considered a facade to hide the coldness that lay within.

Maria had been branded one of those refrigerator moms. When Andre was young, no matter her claims to the contrary, she was blamed for Andre's problems. Rather than being supported in her concern for her son, which is what she craved and needed, she was branded and shunned. At Andre's frequent doctor appointments, the nurses and doctors would stare at her with disdain—almost hatred. While Andre was being evaluated *inside* the clinic room, Maria was made to stand in the hallway *outside* the room, waiting next to the door, completely excluded from his care. Whether the evaluation was short or long, Maria was stuck there—publicly shamed and on display as the cruel monster she was considered to be. Everyone who walked by the clinic room door knew exactly why Maria was there, and they made no secret of their opinions.

In reality, Maria loved her son intensely, and she would do *anything* to help him ... including suffer unjust public humiliation. For Maria, no sacrifice for Andre's sake was too great, no matter the unfairness. So she kept her peace, emotionally died each visit, and showed the strength of Job. And even though she described those experiences as agonizingly humiliating, she told me that the worst part of her suffering was not being allowed to take part in the care and treatment of her child. Shame she could endure. Exclusion broke her heart.

Fortunately, the medical community long ago abandoned this distorted understanding of autism, but some scars still remain.

Maria's experiences happened decades before I talked with her that day, but I could tell from her facial expression and free-flowing tears that for her the memories were still fresh.

In my view, Maria acted like Jesus. For the sake of her child, she "endured [her] cross, scorning its shame" (Heb. 12:2). The undeserved punishment she received, with its prolonged emotional pain and personal humiliation, could not compare to her love of Andre, so she endured time and time again … for *years*. Hers was a sacrificial love, the love of a true mother, so she laid down her life for her son.

As Christians, you and I carry the reputation of Jesus in our lives. Where we go, He goes, and when *we* act, people judge *Him*. That form of judgment is distorted, but it is almost universal. Fair or not, it is everywhere. When we do well, people are drawn to Him. But when we do badly, *He* is shunned—He is told by the very people He loves and for whom He died to wait outside of the "clinic room" of their hearts, because He is blamed for your and my failings, and those people want nothing to do with Him. What breaks Jesus's heart is not a feeling of shame for being identified with our flaws and misdeeds, but for being excluded from those people's hearts when you and I do not live a godly life.

Holiness should not be a part-time hobby in a life focused on other priorities—it should be our strongest desire, not just for the sake of *our* happiness but also for the sake of everyone we meet. Let us pray to live such a godly life.

Much is at stake.

44

Miracles

The strength of our faith does affect the power of our prayers. Scripture states this point categorically. The stronger our faith, the more likely our prayer is going to be answered according to our desires.

But watch out! This truth needs to be carefully understood. There are few dogmas in Christianity more fraught with peril, more misunderstood, or more abused than this one. And I see the abuse of it frequently as a physician. Although this scriptural claim appears simple on the surface, in reality—as is true of so many Christian dogmas—it is not so straightforward. To help explain, although my viewpoint below can apply equally to any type of prayer, I will focus on prayers for healing miracles because of their obvious relevance to my medical professional.

This dogma misunderstood: I have had many patients who, when faced with a serious illness in their own life or in the life of a family member, have been told by fellow Christians that they or their loved one will be healed "if you have strong enough faith, if you believe without doubt. God wants to heal you, but you just have to believe!" (I have heard almost those exact words.) This is a barbaric, brutally distorted understanding of both prayer and of faith, but it is rampant in many churches today. Immeasurable emotional and spiritual harm has been done to faithful believers on account of this perspective—Christians who already are suffering due to illness but now have undeserved guilt added to their pains. Strong faith should *never* be defined as belief without doubt that God will miraculously heal us. Rather, strong faith should be defined by how deeply we are able to love the Lord during our trials and by how extensively we trust Him to do what is best, even when the best is not our choice or not to our understanding.

After all, being convinced that God *can* answer our prayer for healing is not the same as being convinced that God *will* (or should) answer that prayer. What if God's answer to our prayer is no? He would never give such an answer without good reason and much love, even if we do not understand His purposes. Would not our stubborn conviction that God should heal us then pit us directly against Him? Rather than receiving His answer with trust and humility—albeit with deep pain—we would find ourselves expecting our Father to do things our way just because we have convinced ourselves that He will. For example, if I have cancer, these Christians, who typically are comfortably healthy, presume to tell me, "God wants to heal you, but you just have to believe!" But do I know that God wants to heal me? Is that not merely a thinly veiled cover-up for the real truth that *I* want God to heal me?

Furthermore, making my healing dependent upon the strength of *my* conviction, rather than upon God's providence, places far too much importance on my role in the process. If my conviction is absolute, is God obligated to heal me? And if I have some doubt, is God likely to ignore my request? Ironically, such a point of view does not demonstrate more faith in God, but less—our faith would rest not primarily on God but on the strength of our personal conviction. Worst of all, what kind of message does that give to dying patients and to family members who lose a loved one to disease? "Sorry, your faith was not strong enough," implying "It is partly *your* fault that your child is dead." Such a message is not simply wrong; it is cruel.[21]

And where would the viewpoint that absolute confidence brings certain healing logically end? If we could drum up strong enough conviction that God will heal us, would we thereby never succumb to serious illnesses? Never suffer the loss of a loved one? Never die? (At least, until *we* decide that we are ready to die?) One can readily see that this is patent nonsense. If, on the other hand, we understand that prayer is foremost relationship, and that our role (and privilege) is to trust in His providence and wisdom, then we are free to pray for our healing with peace and confidence—God does invite us to ask of Him—but we pray with an understanding that yes and no answers (or "not yet," or "yes, but not in the way you expect", etc.) are equally valid responses to our prayer, and that none of these answers is more or less lovingly given. Additionally, what at first might seem like a no can be a gracious yes that provides something unexpectedly important, even if we realize that it might come to pass after we or our loved ones have died—that is where *ultimate* trust comes into play.

---

[21] Ironically, just a few days after editing this section, I listened to a radio interview of a celebrity singer who described how his mother died of cancer, miserable with self-condemnation, calling herself a failure because she did not have "strong enough faith to be healed." She died full of despair. Angry and embittered at having to watch his mother die that way, this celebrity has rejected the Christian faith, not wanting to have anything to do with a belief system that could promote such an oppressive perspective.

Consider Jesus. If you and I had lived in the year AD 33 and were close relatives of Jesus, would we not have prayed for His deliverance from the Romans? It would have been a compassionate, just, and godly prayer. But what if God had answered that prayer our way? Would it have been for the good of human history? Or even for the good of Jesus? In letting Jesus die—even a death that was brutal and inexplicably unfair by any standard—God's answer to us in the short term would have seemed like a definitive no. And yet God's answer ultimately turned out to be a resounding yes! He did deliver Jesus, but in a form we could not have imagined in the beginning, with benefits we could not have foreseen. Thus at the start, when we had uttered our prayer for Jesus's deliverance, we indeed would not have known best, despite our noble motives. But would we have trusted? Would we have accused God of ignoring our prayer? In our anger and hurt, would we have rejected God for His "lack of compassion"?

That being said, as a father and as a physician, I personally have been involved in tragedies that I cannot—even decades later—understand or explain. These tragedies can appear purely bleak. Neither I nor the people involved, including my own family, might see the greater purpose or the redemption of the suffering during our lifetimes. In such situations, my family, my patients, and I can do naught but cry. It can be heartbreaking, and it is always spiritually confusing, but the patients who have a well-grounded *relationship* with God and who trust in Him regarding calamities that are beyond their understanding, are carried through the pain and can be blessed by God's presence in ways that are astounding. They recognize that rejecting the Lord because of their hardship gains nothing. In the end, God is the only one who can bring any meaning to suffering, the only one who can counter despair, the only one who can take tragedy and somehow bring some good of it. Suffering patients and families who *know* the Lord understand that their ultimate comfort is in the Lord's presence, not in the answer to a specific prayer, and that somehow God hears and knows best and would never have anything but their interests at heart. Although that trust does not provide an immediate answer to the anguished "Why?!!" it does give those Christians hope in their suffering, even when their heart is breaking. Such faith and humility put to shame the hollow "victory-only" mentality of those who insist on a yes answer to their healing prayer.

Faith implies submission, not insistence on one's own way. In the final analysis, the stronger our faith, the *less* insistent we become that God heal us of our illnesses. As our love and trust in God deepen, we are more open to hearing no, not less. "But," one might say, "isn't that backward? We would learn to love and trust God more if He answered our prayer for healing." But would we? It might seem that way during our first health crisis. "If you heal this person, I will trust You forever!" But most of us will have many such crises throughout our lives— in our own health or the health of people we love—each of which might be equally agonizing. For which of those future situations will we find it easier to trust God with any answer other than yes"? For which of the upcoming crises, perhaps the health of a spouse one time followed by the health of a child the next, will we feel less emotionally involved or less desirous of a positive outcome? Indeed, we will want Him to grant healing for each subsequent crisis just as much as for the first. And if we expect Him to answer our prayer for every miracle, will not each successive miracle just reinforce our expectations for the next? Over time, trust will be replaced by presumption. Ironically, in the end we would trust God less, not more. As difficult as it is to accomplish—and I know this firsthand in my own life, both as a father and a physician—we must trust God now, not later.

This dogma understood: At the beginning of this section I claimed, "The stronger our faith, the more likely our prayer is going to be answered according to our desires." But how so? If the above paragraphs detail how people misunderstand this claim, I still am obliged to describe how we *can* properly understand it.

Why is it so, as I believe it is, that God is more likely to answer the prayer for healing from a Christian of stronger faith, such as a Saint? Is God playing favorites? Does He have a secret hierarchy of His children? On the contrary! It is not God's favoritism but human behavior that limits His miracles. The Christian with true strength of faith understands that any healing miracle would be due to God's grace and wisdom, *not* due to the strength of his or her own personal conviction. Ironically, in my view the *less* adamant a Christian becomes that God provide a healing miracle, the *more* God is thereby free to grant the request. What conscientious parent would grant the request of a child who insists on getting his or her way? Giving in to such insistence would be the worst possible lesson for that child. In contrast, hearing the same request from a child who asks with humble deference allows the parents to grant the request in the way all requests should be granted: as a gift, rather than as an acquiescence to presumption.

A Saint asks for miracles with humility, and receiving a healing miracle would not change that Saint's humble spirit. For the believers who insist that they "just have to believe without doubt," a healing miracle simply would affirm their misunderstanding that it was *their own* strong faith that was responsible for the positive answer. At their next church service the same mantra of victory would arise: "See, you just have to believe!" And so goes the message to the next suffering victim. The myth would perpetuate. The oppressive burden on other ill Christians would become worse. And humble trust in and submission to the Lord would diminish.

In the end, the Christian who insists that strong faith means total confidence in getting the answer to prayer that he or she wants does not really have strong faith. God's ultimate purpose for every healing miracle is *always and primarily* to help us grow in faith, not to perform the miracle for its own sake: His highest priority is to heal our souls, not our bodies. Until our most heartfelt request of the Lord during prayer is to grow in love and trust—a request that demonstrates true strength of faith—we can expect little chance of miracles.

45

⚓

Miracles: Further Reflections

Pray for His Presence

In its essence, prayer can be understood as the means by which we come into the presence of the One in whom we have faith, the One we love. Properly practiced, we *meet* God in our prayers; we do not just talk to Him, or hear from Him, or ask of Him. We learn many things while praying, but the first and foremost thing we learn—once we find ourselves in the intimate presence of God—is that nothing is more important or valuable than that very presence ... not even our own healing. Being in God's presence is what we were created for. It is the only thing that can bring ultimate happiness. And when truly in His presence, we find that our prayers change. Our primary and most heartfelt request becomes "Can I have more of your presence?" not "Can you heal me?" The more we know God's intimacy, the more we will want that intimacy above all things. A Christian of stronger faith, who knows this truth, prays *first* for God's presence. And that prayer will always be answered affirmatively.

That being said, our prayer concern often can overwhelm us— something that I personally have experienced many times.

Such a situation occurs, for example, when something dire happens to a family member, at which point our worry is so powerful that even our desire for God's presence is eclipsed. All we can think about is how much we want God to fix whatever is amiss.

Is that bad? Are we, in those moments, in some way being selfish or less than faithful? Not in the least! Appropriate human emotions—such as protective concern for one's children, or love of a spouse or parent—can be overpowering, no matter the level of spiritual maturity. In a time of crisis, our prayer for God's intervention can become a flash flood of words and emotions to God that wash away any other priorities, even the priority of His presence. However, for the Christian of stronger faith this overwhelming prayer comes on the heels of a multitude of prior devotional prayers that have built a strong, loving relationship saturated with trust. In our time of desperation, rather than presumptuously asking for help from a Father to whom we rarely even mumble a haphazard "Good morning," we will be seeking assistance from someone we know intimately—a Father on whose lap we oft have sat and either enjoyed moments of intimacy or cried our hearts out, and a Father whom we trust to do what is best. Even though we emotionally can only contemplate one overwhelming thought—our request—we in reality never will have lost that desire for God's presence. In fact, we will find that we are making our overwhelming plea *in* His presence.

Pray for Peace of Heart

Any Christian, when conditions are comfortable, can have peace of heart. It is during difficult times that the Christian of stronger faith will continue to pray for peace, whereas Christians of weaker faith will fall into the misunderstanding described at the beginning of these reflections on miracles.

When I look into the eyes of my Christian patients who face a health calamity but who still love and trust in the Lord, I see a strength of faith that deeply inspires and moves me. With such saintly patients I openly have cried on many occasions, sharing in their sufferings and also sharing in the peace their prayers bring.

When I look into the eyes of Christian patients who are convinced God is going to heal them because they have "total faith" in God's power of healing, I sense only fear—palpable fear, despite their desperate attempts to hide it. These patients put up a defensive wall I never have been able to penetrate, even if only to empathize with them and say that my heart is with them in their struggles. They cannot allow such empathy. Even the tiniest crack in their 100 percent conviction of upcoming healing means all is lost, so they will not permit compassion to enter in, lest their intrinsic doubts and fears come bubbling to the surface. Besides, what is there to be empathetic about? Victory is at hand! Healing is coming! These patients—decidedly *not* at peace—are so alone and afraid in their suffering. With these patients I also cry … but silently to myself, and for a very different reason.

I have found that Christians' *most fervent* prayers are like windows into their souls, revealing what they most fear in life: Christians whose highest priority is to be healed will put all their conviction into praying for a healing miracle, because what they most fear is death. Christians whose highest priority is love of God will put all their energy into praying for trust, for peace of heart, and for God's presence, because what they most fear is loss of their intimate relationship with the Lord. They strive to lose their fear of death and instead seek God's heart *first*. They do pray for healing, and they are overjoyed if healing occurs, but if they are not healed, then they are like St. Paul, who could say that departing this earth to be with Christ "is better by far" (Philippians 1:23). Give me a choice, and I would choose to be this latter Christian—there is no peace of heart in the former.

46

⚔

In the End ...

Like a kaleidoscope, prayer is multifaceted and infinitely varied. There is no limit to the number of stories that could be told about the subject, with much gain to be had regarding each lesson learned. Nevertheless, the individual details and lessons should not be allowed to obscure the bigger picture. In the end, we must never forget the main reason we pray at all. God does love to hear about and to answer our wishes, and we should bring them to Him with confidence. In fact, I suspect that we vastly underutilize His invitation to present Him with our desires—we should be flooding Him with those concerns. But answering prayer is not God's *primary* role in life. He is not a heavenly bureaucratic functionary whose major purpose is to grant or not grant our requests. God wants something far more important in prayer than just our requests: He wants *us.* God's desperate hope, His undying motive, the reason for all of His sacrifices and patience throughout the millennia, is to fill us with His presence and His purpose, to rescue us from our limitations, and to have us trust in His goodness no matter our situation. He wants us—for our sake, not for His— to *love* Him. Spending time in faithful prayer, building that relationship, dwelling with the Lord in circumstances good or bad, and focusing on Him while presenting our heartfelt desires, is never wasted.

I wish you much fruitful time doing so.

CPSIA information can be obtained
at www.ICGtesting.com
Printed in the USA
FSOW02n1606041116
26982FS